MW01250761

WILLOWDALE

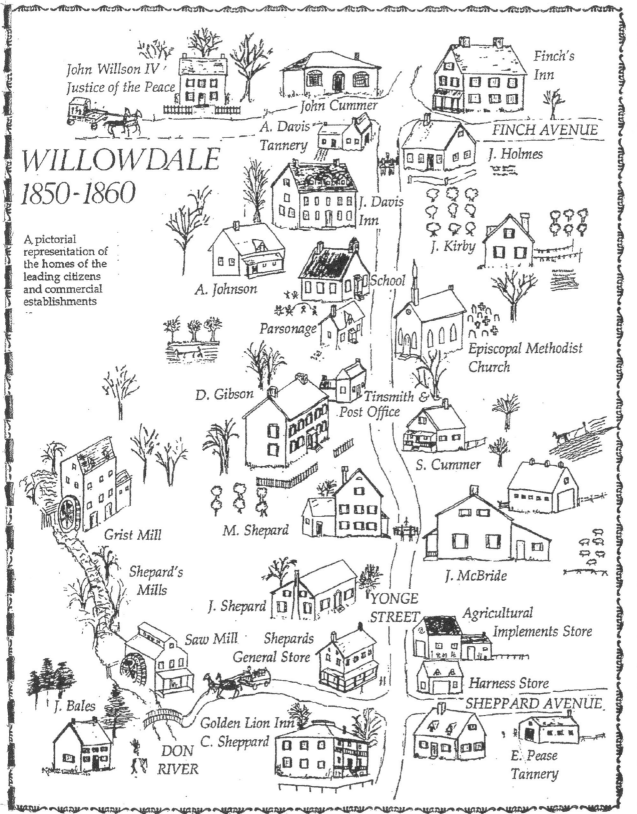

WILLOWDALE
1850-1860

A pictorial representation of the homes of the leading citizens and commercial establishments

John Willson IV Justice of the Peace

John Cummer

A. Davis Tannery

Finch's Inn

FINCH AVENUE

J. Holmes

J. Davis Inn

J. Kirby

A. Johnson

School

Parsonage

Episcopal Methodist Church

D. Gibson

Tinsmith & Post Office

S. Cummer

Grist Mill

Shepard's Mills

M. Shepard

J. McBride

J. Shepard

YONGE STREET

Agricultural Implements Store

Saw Mill

Shepards General Store

Harness Store

J. Bales

Golden Lion Inn C. Sheppard

DON RIVER

SHEPPARD AVENUE

E. Pease Tannery

Courtesy of North York Central Library.

A 19th Century Farming Community in the Heart of North York. *This map comes from a loose-leaf booklet published by the North York Historical Board in 1984. The booklet was researched, written, and designed by Brian Theimer and revised and updated in 1995.*

WILLOWDALE

Yesterday's Farms, Today's Legacy

Scott Kennedy

DUNDURN
TORONTO

Copyright © Scott Kennedy, 2013

All rights reserved. No part of this publication may be reproduced, stored in a retrieval system, or transmitted in any form or by any means, electronic, mechanical, photocopying, recording, or otherwise (except for brief passages for purposes of review) without the prior permission of Dundurn Press. Permission to photocopy should be requested from Access Copyright.

Project Editor: Laura Harris
Editor: Jane Gibson
Copy Editor: Britanie Wilson
Design: Courtney Horner
Printer: Webcom

Library and Archives Canada Cataloguing in Publication

Kennedy, Scott, 1952 February 22-, author
        Willowdale : yesterday's farms, today's legacy / Scott Kennedy

Includes bibliographical references and index.
Issued in print and electronic formats.
ISBN 978-1-4597-1750-3

        1. Willowdale (Toronto, Ont.)--History. 2. Willowdale (Toronto, Ont.)--Biography. I. Title.

FC3097.52 K47 2013   971.3'541   C2013-905481-2
                                                C2013-905482-0

1 2 3 4 5   17 16 15 14 13

We acknowledge the support of the **Canada Council for the Arts** and the **Ontario Arts Council** for our publishing program. We also acknowledge the financial support of the **Government of Canada** through the **Canada Book Fund** and **Livres Canada Books**, and the **Government of Ontario** through the **Ontario Book Publishing Tax Credit** and the **Ontario Media Development Corporation**.

Care has been taken to trace the ownership of copyright material used in this book. The author and the publisher welcome any information enabling them to rectify any references or credits in subsequent editions.

J. Kirk Howard, President

The publisher is not responsible for websites or their content unless they are owned by the publisher.

Printed and bound in Canada.

Visit us at
Dundurn.com | @dundurnpress
Facebook.com/dundurnpress | Pinterest.com/Dundurnpress

Dundurn	Gazelle Book Services Limited	Dundurn
3 Church Street, Suite 500	White Cross Mills	2250 Military Road
Toronto, Ontario, Canada	High Town, Lancaster, England	Tonawanda, NY
M5E 1M2	LA1 4XS	U.S.A. 14150

Cover Image: Holsteins grazing on the south-west corner of Yonge and Steeles in 1957.

To Anne

Contents

Introduction

"If you ate today, thank a farmer"
— SIGN ON A FENCE POST, SOUTH OF PERTH, ONTARIO, JULY 2011

KIDS TAKE EVERYTHING FOR GRANTED. I WAS NO DIFFERENT. Growing up on Toronto's rural fringe, I explored the land and buildings of abandoned farms with more a sense of adventure than a sense of loss. Abandoned barns with buggies suspended from the rafters were more playgrounds than nostalgia to me then, but what I wouldn't give now to tuck my middle-aged brain into my boyhood skin — to go back with a camera and a notebook and at least document what I saw in a respectful fashion.

This book then, must partly be regarded as an apology to the families who worked so hard to build their beautiful farms to feed us all; an apology from a boy on a bike who was more impressed by the bulldozers than what they were bulldozing. We can never go back. Life doesn't flow in that direction. We will never again see fields of grain at the corner of Leslie and Finch or hear the blacksmith's hammer ringing out across Hogg's Hollow, but we can take comfort in the stories and photos of the past, close our eyes and imagine a quieter time.

We can learn to appreciate the lives and accomplishments of these families whose names we may have only seen on street signs or historical plaques, and in so doing, offer our long overdue "thanks."

Each chapter in this book describes either a specific farm or a specific family and follows their stories from the original Crown land grants near the dawn of the nineteenth century to the present day. It is my sincere wish that this book will give readers a new connection to present-day Willowdale and a new appreciation of those who have gone before. It's a lot easier to be stuck in traffic if you know whose farm you are on and can take the time to consider what *they* had to go through to make ends meet.

The name "Willowdale" has defined different areas through different eras. The origins of the name date back to 1855 when David Gibson successfully petitioned the government of Upper Canada for a post office to serve the area around his farm at Yonge Street and Park Home Avenue. He suggested the name "Willow Dale," which was adopted. The area to the north, between Cummer and Steeles Avenues, was referred to as Newtonbrook at this time. In 1866, another post office opened to the south of Willow Dale at the intersection of Yonge Street and Sheppard Avenue. It was called Lansing, as was the community that grew up around it. As time went by, however, postal delivery was streamlined, and by the middle of the twentieth century the

VAUGHAN   MARKHAM

BOROUGH OF NORTH YORK

Courtesy of North York Central Library.

Map of North York with Willowdale highlighted, adapted from the Borough of North York Historical Site Map, circa 1970.

slightly renamed post office of Willowdale was serving the entire area from south of Sheppard to Steeles and from Bathurst Street to Leslie Street. The names Lansing and Newtonbrook continued in use on a localized basis as the whole area gradually came to be known as Willowdale. After the amalgamation of the six separate municipal governments in Metropolitan Toronto into the new City of Toronto in 1998, the post office address for the entire city officially came under the collective name of Toronto.

For the purpose of this book, Willowdale is defined as the area south of Steeles Avenue; north of Highway 401, west of Leslie Street, and east of Bathurst Street. Street names used in these stories are present-day names to allow for an easier visualization of the location of various farms.

The Lives of the Early Settlers and the Birth of North York

There are 44,442 acres in North York, enough for 222 full-sized two-hundred-acre farms. It was a great place for farms, with some of the most fertile land in the world, thanks to the deposits left behind by receding glaciers after the last ice age. The area had seen its fair share of nomadic, aboriginal activity for thousands of years before the first permanent settlements were established at the surprisingly late date of 1400 A.D. French priest and explorer Étienne Brûlé was thought to be the first European to set foot in North York when he travelled down the Humber River, on his way from northern Ontario to Pennsylvania, in September 1615. For the next 170 years or so the only other Europeans would be fur traders and explorers passing through on their way to points north and west. It was not until the late 1700s that any thought was given to permanent white settlement in the area.

As Canadians, much of our time is spent wondering what our neighbours to the south are up to and back then a similar curiosity existed. Lieutenant Governor Simcoe's arrival in 1791 was prompted by Great Britain's desire to understand and maintain the land mass that would one day become Canada. The United States had already fought for and won its independence from the British who had no intention of losing *all* of North America.

John Graves Simcoe was appointed lieutenant governor of Upper Canada in 1791. He immediately had the jurisdiction, known then as the Home District, surveyed and divided into townships and ultimately nineteen separate counties to ensure that local issues would be addressed locally and not by some distant central government.

The Queen's Rangers, which he had commanded during the American Revolution, accompanied Simcoe when he moved the capital of Upper Canada from Newark (Niagara-on-the-Lake) to York (Toronto) in 1792. Early in 1793 he began construction of Yonge Street from Lake Ontario north to the Holland River. This route, named after his friend, the British Secretary of War, Sir George Yonge, was critical to the future of Upper Canada in two ways. First, it was deemed the easiest trade route for reaching the north and west, but it also held great military significance. Hostilities between Great Britain and the United States were always bubbling just below the surface and Simcoe needed a "back door" to the Great Lakes. In the event that battles might erupt on Lake Erie or Lake Ontario, Simcoe wanted a route he could use to sneak up on the enemy from behind and take them by surprise. Yonge Street was central to his plans for preserving Upper Canada as a British colony.

With the West Don River being navigable as far north as Hogg's Hollow in those days, Simcoe decided that the best route to Georgian Bay and the Great Lakes was to use the Don River as far north as Hogg's Hollow, then portage his vessels by wheeled wagons all the way north to the Holland River. Once there they could once again be put in the water to head west to Georgian Bay and Lake Huron. Try to imagine the rigorous task of pulling lake bateaux out of the river in York Mills and then dragging them overland to Holland Landing. Such military moves would be unimaginable today.

The only flaw in this plan was the fact that Yonge Street didn't exist yet, so Simcoe and the Queen's Rangers made it their priority to clear this road through the dense, unforgiving wilderness. This they did, through blackflies, mosquitoes, suffocating heat, and stupefying cold. They did what they intended to do, but as soon as they crossed what became Steeles Avenue, they left the North York of today, and so they leave our story. It had taken them five years to clear Yonge Street from Lake Ontario to Steeles Avenue. Eventually, they would extend Yonge Street all the way to Lake Simcoe. Subsequent extensions would reach Rainy River, near the Manitoba border, and create what is now credited as being the longest street in the world.

With Yonge Street well underway, Simcoe was now able to have surveyors hired to start laying out the concessions, and the lots that became the farms of North York. The grid system used is a beautifully simple one. Basically, the *lot* numbers start from Eglinton Avenue, increasing in numerical value the further north one travels, with Lot 1 being the first lot north of Eglinton and Lot 25 being the first lot south of Steeles. The *concession* numbers are expressed as being either east or west of Yonge Street, so if a lot was the first one north of Eglinton

on the *east* side of Yonge Street, it would be referred to as Lot 1, concession-1E. The first lot north of Eglinton and *west* of Yonge, would be Lot 1, concession-1W. All concessions are a mile-and-a-quarter apart and all lots are one-quarter-of-a-mile wide. Each lot then, measured one-quarter-of-a-mile by one-mile-and-a-quarter, for a total of two hundred acres. Now, with Yonge Street completed and the lots laid out, it was time for Simcoe to start attracting some settlers.

In 1793, he advertised free two-hundred-acre lots to anyone willing to settle in the Township of York. From Simcoe's perspective, the British needed to build a British presence in Upper Canada. In particular, they needed proven Loyalists who would be willing to take up arms to defend their land against incursions from the south. Advertisers and recruiters spread the word throughout Great Britain as well as Nova Scotia and New Brunswick, where many United Empire Loyalists had settled after fighting on the losing side in the American Revolutionary War. While it's nice to think of being given a lot that stretched from Yonge Street to Bayview Avenue for free, the conditions attached to the Crown grants were not to be taken lightly.

To qualify for a grant it was necessary for a prospective settler to prove that he and his family were practising Christians,[1] law-abiding in their home country, and capable of manual labour, but that was just the start. Before settlers were actually granted the deed to their land, they had two years to complete a number of tasks. First, a permanent residence had to be built on the property during the first year, usually a simple log cabin of at least 320 square feet. Next, 10 percent or twenty acres of the land had to be cleared each year, and ten acres of that fenced. Then, the full quarter-mile of forest along both ends of the property had to be cleared for a road allowance thirty-three feet wide and levelled off. This would have to be done with axes, hand-saws, and a team of oxen.

Detail from an archival map of Toronto showing Willowdale with lot numbers and owners' names, from Tremaine's Map of the County of York, *published by George Tremaine in 1860.*

If the settler met all these conditions, the deed to the property was transferred from Crown to settler after two years. If the settler failed to comply, the land stayed with the Crown. Preference was given to military personnel and United Empire Loyalists. Grants of up to 1,200 acres were possible, but presented a formidable task for such applicants, often land speculators with an eye to the future. The more privileged grant recipients were quite within their rights to hire other people to do the dirty work. No one was able to sell their grants, however, until the Crown had transferred the deed to the original owner.

Living conditions must have seemed extremely crude for the first immigrants, many of whom were attached to the military who were leaving older, more-established civilized societies and developed social activities. Their hearts must have sunk when they first laid eyes on that dark, endless forest, thousands of miles from home. Still, they all had their reasons for being here and now had to get to work. There was no turning back now, for if they had never actually experienced winter in Upper Canada before, they had surely heard the stories and realized that the log cabin was clearly a priority.

The first cabins were extremely primitive. Picture one large room with a dirt floor, one fireplace, one door, and one window covered with cloth, shutters, oiled paper, or glass if it was available. The washroom was outside. There was no running water and likely no time for digging a well that first year. Water would have been carried from a nearby creek or spring. Crude, hand-made furniture consisted of a bed, a table, a few chairs, and maybe a cabinet. Improvements to the cabin would have to wait since clearing the land and planting crops for food had to take priority.

The first year, settlers were limited to planting only those crops that could survive in the untilled, stump-riddled soil. Potatoes, pumpkins, onions, squash, corn, peas, and turnips were popular choices. The settlers' diet was supplemented by hunting and fishing as back then pheasants, partridges, deer, trout, and salmon were plentiful in North York. Wild berries and other wild fruits were a welcome addition to the diet. Bears and wolves were also quite common so caution was required when out and about.

Logs left over from clearing the land were piled up and burned. The remaining wood was re-piled and burned again. The resulting ashes were taken to an ashery to be made into potash, which was used in the manufacture of soap, glass, dyes, and baking soda. Cash was still rare so the settlers would exchange their ashes for cloth, tea, whisky, flour, or root vegetables to get them through that first winter. The Crown also donated supplies to the earliest settlers but the availability of these government supplies was so notoriously unreliable that most settlers would only turn to the Crown in times of imminent starvation.

Pioneer families were much less mobile than the generations that came later. Neighbours were literally few and far between. One house or cabin would commonly house several generations of one family. Social interaction was pretty much limited to the communal "bees," when settlers would get together to pool their resources and abilities. There were land-clearing bees, logging bees, husking bees, quilting bees, cabin-raisings, barn-raisings, and many other tasks that were accomplished more easily as more neighbours became involved. After the work was done, they would share a meal, followed by a little fiddle music, dancing, and perhaps a jug or two of whisky. When the first churches were built, they too would become centres of social activity. All such get-togethers were much appreciated by the settlers as a welcome break from their gruelling routines.

Assuming survival of that first winter, the first spring would involve learning the magic of maple-syrup production — not for the syrup itself but for the maple sugar that could be made from it. (The cane sugar used today was simply not available in Upper Canada back then.) The various First Nations tribes who had been tapping maple trees for generations willingly shared their knowledge with the settlers. To repay this kindness, settlers would often give iron kettles to the Natives, which made boiling and processing the sap much easier than had been the case with the earlier wooden vessels.

Another improvement in the second year would be a well. This would be dug near the cabin for convenience and capped off with a stone or wooden enclosure to keep children and animals from falling in. Trips to the creek or the spring were now a thing of the past, and, although pumps would not be widely available until the 1860s, it was still a great convenience to pull as much water as needed out of the nearby well with ropes and buckets.

Mills were also built in the second or third year of settlement. If sheer luck or sufficient forward-thinking provided a strong-running stream or river on the property, building a sawmill and/or a gristmill became a possibility. Sawmills were simpler and smaller since they didn't require the large, heavy mill stones of the gristmill. Generally, mills were helpful in a number of ways, allowing millers to process their own raw materials, either for barter or personal use, as well as providing a place for neighbouring settlers to have their goods processed. In this latter case, the miller would keep a percentage of the flour or lumber as payment, and the neighbour would go home with finished goods without laying out any cash. It was also quite common for a distillery to be attached to a gristmill. The distilleries used the smaller, inferior grain or "trailings" to make whisky, a beverage highly prized for its ability to soften the hard edges of pioneer life.

This was also the time to start thinking about some domestic animals, probably a cow and some chickens to start with — a source of eggs, milk, and homemade butter. The following years would see the arrival of more cows and chickens as well as ducks, geese, sheep, and turkeys. This would require fencing and coops for the poultry to protect them from the local wildlife. Hogs were also raised but were generally allowed to run free until hunted like wild game in the fall.

Autumn was slaughtering time, when the abattoirs, tanneries, and smokehouses would swing into action. Here again, the barter system prevailed, so farmers with no money could go home with tanned leather and smoked meats and the tanners and slaughtermen would end up with meat and leather of their own, taken as payment for their services.

The stumps left behind after the land was cleared could take up to ten years to rot away completely, but early settlers needed tillable land sooner than that so they kept at the stumps with their oxen to clear as much land as they could. Then they would plant their first grain crops, usually wheat, rye, buckwheat, barley, or oats. Flax was also a valuable early crop with most farms featuring at least one acre of this most versatile plant with its beautiful blue flowers. The settlers grew flax to make cloth for their own clothes. The almost unbelievably labour-intensive process involved rolling the uprooted plants in water for several weeks before drying and pounding them. They were then flayed and combed to remove the flax fibres from the stalks. The fibres were then spun, woven, and sewn into clothes that would seem extremely crude to us today. Back then, however, they were just fine.

More new tools were available every year. Shovels, pitchforks, rakes, a plough, axes, saws, and scythes had to be acquired, and the little log cabin made a bit more civilized. A room divider on the main floor was a popular method of providing a little privacy, as was the construction of a second-floor bedroom. A cellar was another improvement that could pay many dividends, for although the labour required to dig a cellar out by hand was not for the faint of heart, the results were substantial. Carrots, turnips, onions, and potatoes could be stored there where they would stay fresh for most of the winter. The extra storage space was also a bonus since a proper barn probably didn't exist yet. Primitive lean-tos were often constructed for animals before a barn was built. The cellar was a place to store all new tools as well as flax, cloth, firewood, and flour.

Cisterns were another popular and practical addition to the cellar. These were large water storage tanks made from wood or cement that stored captured rainwater. When hand pumps became available, they made cisterns even more attractive, as now water could be pumped from the cellar to the kitchen. With a proper wood floor for the cabin now in place, the prospect of a second winter is starting to look a lot better than the first.

Despite all of these improvements, life was still pretty primitive. Baths were taken outside in the warmer months and in the kitchen area in front of the fireplace during wintertime, in the same metal tub. The well-water was heated on the hearth. The whole family commonly used the same water and the soap that they had made themselves from potash and animal fat.

Interior lighting was uninspiring. There were few options, none of them all that satisfactory. There were candles made from animal fat, which smelled terrible, dripped, required constant trimming, and didn't throw much light. Pine knots could be burned on flat stones, or grease lamps, pan lamps or fat lamps lit, none of which were terribly effective. The best bet would probably have been candlewood — splints cut from the heart of pine or fir logs, which were stuck in holders and lit just like candles. They burned steadily, needed no trimming, were brighter than candles, and even smelled nice. However, there weren't any matches yet. If the fire went out, it was off to the neighbours' for a bucket of hot embers or better still, a handily available tinderbox. The tinderbox was a metal cylinder that contained a piece of quartz flint, a piece of iron on which to strike the flint, and some tinder. The tinder could be any flammable material, usually a piece of pre-scorched cloth

or linen. The flint was struck on the iron until a spark ignited the tinder. This process could take up to half-an-hour.

By the 1820s, bright, clean-burning wax candles were available at most general stores. Shortly afterwards, effective lamps with cloth wicks and turpentine or alcohol-based fuels also became available. By 1856, Ezra Butler Eddy was making the first matches in Canada at his factory in Hull. Kerosene lamps became popular in the 1860s. Finally, electricity would reach into rural Upper Canada in the 1900s. Until then, nighttime was best left for sleeping.

By the second year, more trees would be tapped, more sap boiled, and more maple sugar made. Each subsequent year would see an increase in activity, — clearing more land and pulling more stumps, planting more crops, and raising more livestock.

In a few more years, actual income would become a reality. As the Town of York, which was changed by provincial legislation to the City of Toronto on March 6, 1834, grew to the south, it would need ever-increasing amounts of grain, lumber, flour, meat, fruit, milk, and vegetables. The roads grew steadily from stump-riddled, muddy trails to passable, functional routes that could actually be used to convey goods to market in the city.

Commercial agriculture, as it is known today, didn't really exist until the 1820s. What a sense of pride the first farmers must have shared at this juncture — to have survived those gruelling early years, to finally get their deeds from the Crown, to see their children born at home, grow into strong knowledgeable partners, and to see the farms become profitable enterprises. Now it was time for a new house.

The cabin, by now far too small for a growing family, would be used as a stable, storage area, or lodging for hired hands. The new house would be frame, brick, or stone, depending on the availability of raw materials and the skills of the local craftsmen who were available and willing to pitch in. The house would be built with the help of neighbours, likely starting with a day-long framing bee, and completed piece-by-piece as time and finances allowed. Around the same time a new barn would be needed, again built during a barn-raising with the help of neighbours, a communal practice that involved everyone. The barn would house livestock, farm implements, hay, straw, a wagon, a sleigh, and maybe even a buggy, as the roads were now smooth enough to be used by horse-drawn vehicles. The wagon would be used for chores around the farm and to take goods to market. If fortunate enough to have a buggy, it would be used to take the family to church and social events or, with some trepidation, lent to the eldest to go "a-courtin.'" With roads now passable for buggies, wagons, and stagecoaches, and both branches of the Don River still navigable as far south as Lake Ontario, export markets began to open up.

Orchards were now being planted on newly cleared land, making a pleasant addition to the settlers' diet when the trees began to bear fruit. Apples, pears, peaches, plums, and cherries were sold fresh as well as being preserved for the winter or made into jams, jellies, pies, and tarts. Apples were especially prized for their versatility as they could be turned into pies, preserves, apple sauce, apple butter, apple cider (alcoholic or not), vinegar, or simply stored and eaten raw.

As the early pioneers moved into their fifties or sixties, they remained actively involved in running their farms, happy to see their children and grandchildren stepping up to make sure that the family was able to take advantage of emerging new opportunities. After all, for most, that was the reason for immigrating — to see their children owning their own land, and controlling their own destiny, not under anyone's thumb.

By the last half of the 1800s, things began to evolve more quickly as the Industrial Revolution took hold in Europe, Great Britain, and the cities of North America. With change came the need to adapt. Potash was no longer needed, since by 1850 reserves were discovered and mined in Germany. The wheat and flour from Upper Canada would be replaced in the international marketplace by wheat from Manitoba, Saskatchewan, and Alberta, as those areas were opened up to settlement and farming. Manufactured goods were now more readily available to North York farmers now that the improved roads, which eased the transport of goods to the rest of the world, ran both ways, and the general stores of North York were full of desirable modern conveniences.

Farmers suddenly found themselves depending on cash. The focus shifted from doing, making, or growing what was *needed*, to selling enough goods to other people to get the cash to buy what was *wanted*. Even though most settlers were now well-fed, sheltered, and fulfilled in their endeavours, who could say no to cleaner, brighter candles, or a more efficient stove, a new reaper for harvesting grain, or softer, more durable clothes? And so was born our consumer society.

By this time, livestock production was the fastest growing type of agriculture in North York. With much more land now cleared for livestock food production and grazing, herds of purebred beef and dairy cattle such as Aberdeen Angus, Ayrshire, Herefords, Holsteins, Gurnseys, and Jerseys became a common sight. Many of the cattle were raised for export as breeding stock and beef-on-the-hoof. As might be expected, dairy products were also making up a significant portion of farm income by the time the nineteenth century drew to a close. Advances in transportation and cold storage now made it possible to ship such perishable commodities farther than ever before. Most successful farms would now have some sort of ice house, a small stone or wooden structure in a cool shady spot where blocks of ice that had been cut from a nearby lake or river in the winter were insulated with straw or sawdust. The resulting situation would have been sufficient to keep milk, cheese, butter, meat, and eggs fresher for much longer than ever before. Ultimately, the best hedge against fluctuations in market prices and customer demand would prove to be a well-balanced mixed farm where grains, fruit, vegetables, lumber, maple syrup, meat, and dairy products all accounted for a percentage of the farms' income.

The twentieth century brought many changes to North York. As already noticed, the most exceptional change was probably the vast improvement in transportation. Where a century earlier the roads had been muddy, uneven, and stump-riddled, they were now flat and surfaced in crushed stone, hard-packed dirt, or even pavement. Electric transit cars called radials ran all the way up Yonge Street to Lake Simcoe. The first automobiles, trucks, and gasoline-powered farm vehicles were starting to appear. Rail lines now ran through North York, offering a reliable, inexpensive way to ship products to far-away markets.

Electricity was common in the city now and reaching further into the country all the time. These were the glory years for the farmers of North York. The brutally primitive conditions of the early pioneer days were part of a now-distant past. The burgeoning markets of Toronto and other nearby cities needed more food all the time. Social and educational situations were vastly improved. For the next fifty years, any farmer in the world would have been happy to have a farm in North York. There was only one real problem, and it would be addressed rather swiftly in 1922.

The problem was that North York didn't actually *exist* until 1922. Prior to that, the area had simply been another part of the Township of York, but as the twentieth century progressed the farmers found themselves increasingly marginalized as municipal council ignored their concerns to focus on Toronto's urban issues. In 1915, there was only one farmer left on council. By 1919 there were none, despite the fact that the farmers were paying nearly 25 percent of the taxes collected by the township.

In 1921, farmers James Muirhead, W.J. Buchanan, Roy Risebrough, W.C. Snider, and John Brummel criss-crossed the area in Roy's new-fangled Model T Ford, collecting signatures for a petition requesting secession from York. The Private Bills Committee of the Ontario Legislature heard the application in 1921, and the only thing that delayed a vote on the matter was the fact that other farmers to the south of the proposed area wanted to be included in the new jurisdiction as well. After the boundaries were redrawn to include this new group, the bill was passed on June 13, 1922. The Township of North York was incorporated as a separate municipality on July 18 of the same year, with a population of less than 6,000 people.

When the inaugural council was elected on August 12, it was comprised of Reeve R.F. Hicks, Deputy-reeves/Councillors Oliver Bales, James Muirhead, W.G. Scrace, and Councillor W.J. Buchanan. Roy Risebrough was appointed police chief and sole constable in a force of one. The secession came in the nick of time as North York was soon to be swamped by a tide of unprecedented and unimaginable population growth.

It must be difficult for newer residents to imagine what North York looked like back then. There was no Highway 401, no Don Valley Parkway, no buses, or subways. Bayview and Leslie were two-lane dirt roads. Steam locomotives pulled trains of wooden boxcars across level crossings. Don Mills Road only went as far north as York Mills Road. Giant elm trees dotted the landscape, looking almost African with their tall bare trunks and broad high canopies, visible in old photos but no longer part of the current landscape.

There were no buildings higher than three or four storeys, and they were usually barns or silos. Horses, buggies, and wagons were the preferred means of transportation, sharing the rural routes with early motor cars. The air was clean and smelled of hay, grass, livestock, wood smoke, pine, earth, and wildflowers. There was so little light pollution that you could see the Northern Lights. Imagine that! As late as the early 1960s, people could see the Northern Lights in North York from the corner of Bayview and Sheppard. Anyone hiking north or east from Bayview and Sheppard in the 1950s and early 1960s would have seen nothing but woods, farms, fields, and the occasional country house or rural gas station. People fished and swam in the Don River.

This census listing provides some idea of just how overwhelming the growth of North York has been:

POPULATION GROWTH IN NORTH YORK
FROM 1923 TO 1991

1923	6,303
1933	13,964
1943	24,528
1953	110,311
1963	303,577
1971	504,150
1981	559,520
1991	563,290

Growth before the end of the Second World War was significant but fairly measured, as the population came close to doubling every ten years. The vast majority of this growth occurred in the two concessions east and west of Yonge Street, since Yonge was the only street with any regular public transit to carry new residents to work in downtown Toronto.

After the Second World War, however, all kinds of hell broke loose as the baby boom burst the dam and flooded upwards and outwards. According to the table above, nearly *five times* as many people were living in North York in 1953

as had been living there a scant ten years earlier. After that, roughly 200,000 people would move to North York every ten years until the growth finally slowed somewhat around 1980. The three decades that followed the war years would mark the end of farming in North York.

Residential and commercial growth was everywhere and municipal taxes were rising at an alarming rate, to the point where fewer and fewer farmers could even afford to stay on their own land. Farms east and west of Yonge Street, from Victoria Park to the Humber River, and as far north as Steeles Avenue, fell like dominoes. By the autumn of 1969 there were only a few isolated farmers still harvesting crops — men such as Fred Hampson, who farmed his own land, as well as land he rented from the Myers family at the corner of Don Mills Road and Finch Avenue. A few years later, it was all over.

It was a strange time to live through since a way of life was being erased before people's very eyes, and yet most newer residents viewed this as a good thing. Progress was viewed as good. Clinging to the past was bad. Tear down those messy old barns, build some beautiful new high-rises, create some more roads, more stores, more cars, and more street lights. In the fifties, sixties, and seventies, historical preservation wasn't really a part of the equation. Out with the old. Newer is better. It was a philosophy of life that left no room for farmers or their "old" ways. So now they are all gone, all of the farms and the farmers of North York, but, fortunately, street names and other traces of their existence remain behind.

This is the story of those early farm families who built Willowdale, one that recognizes their contributions to the history of North York, and to the history of Toronto — an opportunity to view the past to better understand the present. Closing your eyes and remembering their stories allows you to become part of the story too. You are now part of the journey to the early days of Willowdale.

CHAPTER ONE

The Shepards:
Joseph and Catherine

OF ALL THE PIONEER NAMES IN THIS BOOK, NONE RESONATE more with present-day Torontonians than this one does. The east-west artery named after this earliest of pioneer families is one of the busiest and most talked about in the city. Sheppard Avenue (as was common then, both spellings, Shepard and Sheppard, are found in the records) runs all the way from the Humber River in the west to the Rouge River in the east. Like its neighbour to the south, Lawrence Avenue, also named for a pioneer family, Sheppard Avenue spans virtually the entire city. A major transportation corridor, as well as a magnet for development, it is seldom out of the news — a fitting legacy for patriarch Joseph Shepard, who traversed this land on a regular basis in a time before white settlement.

Joseph's early days are cloaked in mystery, owing to the destruction of many records around the time of the Revolutionary War in the United States, but it seems he was born in New Hampshire to Irish immigrant parents, on August 10, 1765. Mozart was nine years old and had already spent over three years performing in the palaces and concert halls of Europe. Joseph Shepard — while precocious in his own way — would prove a much later bloomer. In 1774, when Beethoven was turning four, the Shepards moved to Upper Canada, apparently settling in the Bay of Quinte area. They were Loyalists and likely felt uncomfortable living south of the border, as the potential of armed conflict with Britain became ever more likely.

Sporadic mentions of Joseph appear during the late 1700s, but it's hard to know who to believe. The *Globe* newspaper of April 26, 1899, reported that he came to North York in 1785 to travel with Native traders, as he had done in the Quinte area. This seems quite likely, as Joseph would be twenty years old by then, and practised in the physical challenges that travelling with Natives on their trading routes demanded. The next we hear of Joseph is that he apparently applied for and received a land grant in Kingston in 1790 that he did not accept. His permanent relationship with North York would begin three years later.

By 1793, Joseph Shepard was helping the very first white settlers in the area to erect their initial primitive log cabins. In 1798, after helping the others with their shanties, Joseph built his own cabin on the northwest corner of present-day Yonge and Sheppard. In 1802, he bought the lot where his cabin stood from a William Dickson, who had acquired this Lot 16-1W (on the north side of Sheppard, running west from Yonge Street to Bathurst) in 1798, a year after it had been granted to James Johnson. It was still mostly forest when Joseph purchased it.

On April 11, 1803, Joseph married Catherine Fisher, a member of the Pennsylvania German family, led by patriarch Jacob Fisher, who had come to Upper Canada in 1796 and settled near what today is Dufferin and Steeles after receiving a land grant from the Crown. The Fishers were accompanied on their move by Jacob Kummer (later to become Cummer), who had married Catherine's sister, Elizabeth, when the families lived in Pennsylvania. The Fisher family farmed, constructed mills, opened a blacksmith shop, and soon a little village named Fisherville was born at the crossroads. The Fisherville Presbyterian Church, constructed in 1856, was moved to Black Creek Pioneer Village in 1960, where it can still receive visitors.

At present-day Yonge and Sheppard, Joseph and Catherine were wasting little time starting their family. Their first child, Thomas, was born in 1804, followed by three other sons and four daughters. In 1805, Joseph applied for and was granted the deed to Lot 17-1W, directly north of the family's first farm, giving them all a little something to look forward to and some room to grow.

The Shepards' days were now defined by hard labour and incremental progress — clearing land, burning the stumps, selling the potash, planting whatever they could, raising some livestock, raising a family, and making their cabin more comfortable. The latter two responsibilities would have fallen almost exclusively to Catherine. Joseph, still as involved and gregarious as ever, somehow found time to serve York Township in a number of appointed and elected positions. Beginning in 1804, he was township assessor for three terms and pound-keeper for two, which, in those days, included more lost and errant horses, swine, and cattle than cats and dogs. He was also elected overseer of highways and fence-viewer.

Both these latter positions had the potential to put Joseph in frequent conflict with his neighbours. As an overseer of highways, he had to make sure that the settlers were clearing the road allowances around their farms as per the conditions of their Crown land grant applications and take action if they were negligent. As a fence-viewer, he was obliged to settle disputes among neighbouring farmers with respect to livestock caught wandering onto other peoples' farms. At the time, hogs and cattle were marked for identification, but allowed to graze at large in the country. When they were caught "trespassing" on fenced land, they were impounded by the landowner and the fence viewer was called in to make sure that the fences on the property met the township specifications that had been designed to keep the wandering livestock out. As can be imagined, this would have sparked many a heated argument that Joseph would have had to settle in such a way that all parties, Joseph included, would be able to continue living as neighbours on good terms.

In 1807, Joseph took his political involvement to the next level when he allied himself with the fledgling reform movement in Upper Canada, which was beginning to speak out against injustices the farmers believed themselves to be suffering at the hands of the ruling Family Compact. The farmers felt that the Family Compact, who controlled the government through their closed network of entitled families, were guilty of corruption, land speculation, religious favouritism, and administrative extravagance. That year, Joseph chaired meetings to support Robert Thorpe, a judge of the Court of the King's Bench in Upper Canada, in his campaign to make the Family Compact more accountable. Though the reform movement wasn't really organized until the 1820s, Joseph stood for election to Upper Canada's lower house, running on a reform platform. A split in the reform vote led to his defeat by the government candidate, Thomas Ridout, who had already served as sergeant-at-arms to the House of the Assembly and clerk of the peace for the Home District.

To some, Joseph Shepard was an unlikely reformer since he was a supporter of the Church of England (Anglican), an allegiance usually accompanied by Loyalist tendencies, and, in fact, he did fight with the British troops in the War of 1812 as a forty-seven-year-old private in the 3rd York Militia. He was seriously wounded at the Battle of York in April 1813 when the powder magazine at Fork York was intentionally blown up to prevent it from falling into the hands of the American invaders. Catherine found him the next morning, unconscious and lying in his own dried blood. His injuries, including broken ribs and a mangled left thigh, were serious enough to warrant a lifetime pension. In addition, he was given one hundred acres in Tecumseth Township in Simcoe County in appreciation for his service.

Meanwhile, back on the farm, the Shepards' four hundred acres were becoming more productive every year. As more land was cleared, more crops were planted, more livestock was introduced, and orchards began to bear fruit. The farm was becoming quite a profitable enterprise. By all accounts, Joseph was a man with a social conscience who believed in sharing any good fortune that might come his way, a trait he may well have absorbed from the Natives he travelled with in his youth, who believed in re-paying kindness with kindness. In keeping with Joseph's values, he and Catherine gifted the community with a parcel of land that continues to benefit local residents to this day when they bought two-and-three-quarters acres of tableland on the east side of Yonge Street, half-a-mile north of York Mills, and donated the land for the construction of the new St. John's Anglican Church. Joseph himself worked alongside other members of the congregation, felling the virgin timber on site and squaring the logs with axe and adze.

In the 1820s, Joseph built a sawmill and a gristmill on the West Don River that ran through the western portion of his farm near Bathurst Street, in an area that came to be known as Chuckle Hollow. The mills were run by his sons, and, like most mills in pioneer North York, they were very profitable enterprises. Joseph remained committed to the reform movement and especially to its leader, William Lyon Mackenzie, whom he had supported in Upper Canada's election of 1832. Two years later, the Town of York reverted to its original First Nations' name of "Toronto," and Mackenzie was elected the town's first mayor. This was also the year that the Shepards would really start to spread their wings.

In 1834, Joseph and Catherine's two eldest sons bought farms of their own in the second concession west of Yonge Street. Thomas, now thirty years old, bought Lot 18-2W, which ran east from Bathurst Street to Dufferin Street, about halfway between Sheppard and Finch. The eastern portion of his farm included the majestic sweep of the West Don Valley where the Holocaust Education and Memorial Centre of Toronto stand today, just north of Bathurst and Sheppard. Jacob, a couple of years younger than Thomas, bought Lot 19-2W, directly to the north of his brother's farm. Both sons built new mills on the West Don River and got down to the serious business of building their own farms. Back on the original farm at Yonge and Sheppard, Joseph and Catherine were about to start construction of a house to replace their log cabin — a house that is still a home today, on its original foundation, over 175 years later.

Joseph was now nearly seventy years old, but he still had his eye on the future when he decided to embark on the daunting task of constructing a new farmhouse for his family. He did a fabulous job, since even now the home is one of North York's real treasures. Anne M. de Fort-Menares, former architectural historian to the City of North York, described

Photo by Lorna Gardner, North York Historical Society, NYHS 1286.

The much-admired home of Joseph Shepard, built circa 1835 on what is today's Burndale Avenue, is shown here as it appeared in 1968.

the house as one of a group of "Small frame houses of exceptional finesse...." in the January 1985 edition of the *Canadian Collector*.[1] Though surrounded today by the more pedestrian dwellings that were erected on its former farmland, the Shepard house still manages to charm.

The storey-and-a-half clapboard structure delivers all of the elegance and symmetry that its mix of late-Georgian and neo-classical Loyalist styles could only suggest. Simple, genteel, and dignified, the house offers a glimpse of a style not often seen in Toronto, where Loyalist flourishes are rare.[2] Appearing small from the outside, the centre hall layout provides an interior of surprising accommodation. Throughout the home, attention to detail elevates the simple to the sublime.

The front door case, easily the most striking feature of the house, is a complicated piece of work that at first glance appears quite wide for the overall size of the house. And yet, the meticulous attention to detail and proportion somehow manages to merge the grand and the humble in such a way that both seem completely satisfied. The recessed, six-panel door is bracketed by wide sidelights with six-over-four sliding sash windows. Four fluted Doric-style pilasters surround the door and sidelights, which originally stood alone without a transom or fanlight. Alterations by subsequent owners have added a pediment, dentils, and other embellishments, which might charitably be described as "gilding the lily."

The quality of the woodwork is almost certainly attributable to the Shepards' sawmills, which were now able to produce the type of millwork that Joseph and Catherine may only have dreamed of when they built their log cabin. Similarly, the many panes of glass that graced their new home would have been unobtainable thirty years earlier when the stump-riddled roads made transportation of glass an unlikely prospect. Interior decoration, while simple and unpretentious, continued to demonstrate fastidious attention to detail. Formal doorframes were decorated with hand-carved rosettes. Sensuous, well-figured newel posts almost dared you *not* to touch them, while reverse cyma curves seamlessly connected the tread of one stair to the next.

The house would remain in the family until 1912 when the farm began to be subdivided. Fortunately, both the years and subsequent owners have been kind, and the house has been able to absorb modern additions such as hydro, a furnace, and a washroom without losing its integrity. Located at 90 Burndale Avenue, the house defiantly faces east to Yonge Street, while its modern neighbours all face north or south.

Joseph would only enjoy his new house for a couple of years. He died on May 3, 1837, at the age of seventy-one. He had worked hard and achieved much since he first laid eyes on the virgin forests of Upper Canada more than fifty years earlier. Now it was up to the rest of the family to carry on without him. They were about to live through the most dangerous year of their lives.

In 1837, Joseph's good friend, William Lyon Mackenzie, set the wheels in motion that would lead to the Upper Canada Rebellion. More will be said about the rebellion and these early farmers, as will be seen in later chapters, but here the focus is on the considerable involvement by the Shepard family.

All four sons were Reformers. They offered the relative isolation of the corners of their farms, which were sheltered in the valley of the West Don River, as a training ground for the Reform soldiers, and space in their mills for the manufacture of ammunition. When the time came to actually confront the government troops in early December, all the brothers were on the front lines. Their mother, Catherine, also played a major role on more than one occasion.

On December 4, approximately fifty Reformers from the north stopped in at the Shepards' house for a little warmth and nourishment on their way down Yonge Street to engage the government troops. Catherine was only too happy to provide them with what she could. When the fateful day of December 7 came, Jacob and Joseph II were at Montgomery's Tavern where they fought alongside the woefully inept William Lyon Mackenzie. Their rag-tag group of rebels was quickly routed by the better-equipped government troops in a battle that lasted less than an hour. Jacob and Joseph were captured and imprisoned in the Toronto jail.

The rebel leader William Lyon Mackenzie was so inept that he left his carpet bag behind when he fled Montgomery's Tavern — his bag that contained a list of the names and addresses of every single one of his supporters. Discovered by the government troops before they burned the tavern to the ground, the bag made their next few days a whole lot easier.

Michael and Thomas Shepard led the government troops on a much merrier chase than their brothers. On the morning of December 7, they were far from Montgomery's Tavern with a group of several hundred well-armed rebels. Commanded by Colonel Peter Matthews, they had been charged with the capture of the bridge over the Don River at King Street from the defending government troops. In this instance, it was the rebels who nearly carried the day, but, while they were able to set fire to the bridge, they did not destroy it. When news reached them that the tavern had fallen and the rebellion was lost, Michael and Thomas made it as far as the Humber River before they were captured and imprisoned in the same jail that already held their brothers. While there, they witnessed the executions of Colonel Matthews and Samuel Lount, one of the rebels who had stopped at Catherine's house on December 4. Both men were hanged.

Catherine was again forced into action on the night of the rebellion when government troops burst into her house looking for rebels. The troops went from room to room, slashing quilts and pillows, and stabbing beds with their swords. As they left each bedroom, they set the mattresses on fire. Catherine followed frantically, dousing the blazes as best she could, trying to save her barely two-year-old home.

Despite Catherine's best efforts, one rebel commander *was* captured there that night. Colonel Anthony Van Egmond, the commander from the Huron Tract, who had opened the Huron Road for the Canada Company in 1828, had fled on horseback, heading north up Yonge Street along with rebel leader William Lyon Mackenzie after the battle at Montgomery's Tavern. Once they reached The Golden Lion Hotel, at today's Yonge and Sheppard, with government troops hot on their heels, the two men split up. Mackenzie exchanged his horse for a fresh one at the hotel and headed west to the farms of Thomas and Jacob Shepard at Bathurst Street. Colonel Egmond, a much

older man, was by now completely exhausted from the battle and pursuit and sought shelter at the much closer home of Catherine Shepard. He was captured there by government troops and imprisoned in the Toronto jail, where he contracted pneumonia and died the following January.

What a cold, hellish night it must have been, as soldiers set fire to surveyor David Gibson's house on the lot directly to the north of the Shepard farm, and other homes in the area as well. (The current Gibson House was built in the 1850s to replace this one that was burned by the troops.) When the sun came up on December 8, Catherine could actually count herself among the lucky ones, as she still had a roof over her head, although apparently there are still charred rafters in the house as mute testimony to what happened that night.

In the days following the rebellion, government troops scoured the back roads on horseback, burning farmhouses to smoke out any remaining rebels, no doubt aided in their search by William Lyon Mackenzie's little black book. In addition to the government troops, local farmers had to fear roving gangs of civilian, vigilante Loyalists who, with full government support, fanned out across North York, looting and burning buildings and assaulting or capturing any of their neighbours they suspected of being sympathetic to the rebel cause. In the aftermath of this all-out assault, the four Shepard boys suffered disparate fates.

Jacob and Joseph II were held in custody until May 12, 1838, when they were released and allowed to return home. Thomas and Michael were not so lucky. Six months after they were captured, they still hadn't been brought to trial. Nonetheless, they were sent to Kingston to await banishment to Van Dieman's Land (Tasmania). Realizing that they would never see Upper Canada again if sent into exile, they escaped from custody, using the cover of a massive nighttime thunderstorm to mask their escape. They knelt and prayed in the pouring rain before splitting up and running for their lives. Miraculously, they both found themselves in the United States a little over a week later, where they were welcomed as heroes for fighting the British troops. Their families crossed Lake Ontario to visit them in Lewiston for what they thought might have been one last time. The brothers then set out to find work while their families returned to North York. Three years later, word reached Thomas and Michael that they had been pardoned and were now free to return to Upper Canada. They didn't have to be told a second time.

Thomas returned to the farm he had purchased in 1834, while Michael returned to the farm he had inherited from his father in 1837. It seems that Joseph was fair to the end. Realizing that his two eldest sons were now successfully farming and milling on their own properties, he left his own two farms to his two *youngest* sons, Michael and Joseph II. Joseph II inherited the farm where his mother Catherine still lived while Michael inherited Lot 17-1W, directly to the north. Joseph II and his family moved into Catherine's farmhouse where they remained until 1860.

Thomas's farm and mills were extremely productive. The farmland produced livestock and grain, as well as fruit from three acres of excellent orchards. His steam-powered sawmill was capable of cutting 4,000 feet of lumber per day and the flour he produced was sold as far away as Montreal, but his farm had one serious flaw. It seems that the hills into the valley where his mills stood were so steep that the roads became virtually impassable when rain or snow turned them to mud. At times like these, not even a team of oxen could haul a wagonload out of the valley, so Thomas would carry the one-hundred-pound bags of flour up the hill on his shoulders, one at a time, in order to satisfy his customers and get his product to market. In 1847, he offered the farm for sale but found no takers and went back to work. The Shepard brothers' next series of land transactions would make a drunken game of musical chairs seem organized.

In 1849, Joseph II was granted thirty-eight acres of Lot 15-3E on the southeast corner of today's Leslie and Sheppard where George S. Henry's Oriole Lodge Farm would one day stand. In 1852, he sold the parcel to his brother Michael, who bought thirty-three acres of Lot 14-3E directly to the south at the same time, and built a sawmill on the East Don River that ran through his new holdings. The operation was a profitable enterprise, processing over 50,000 feet of lumber a month and employing two people. In 1856, Thomas was finally able to sell the farm with the steep hills. The buyer was none other than his younger brother, Joseph II, who had just sold his property at Leslie and Sheppard to Michael. Thomas then turned around and bought Michael's farm and sawmill in Oriole. Michael then returned to Yonge and Sheppard to farm the lot his father had left him in 1837. Thomas soon added a gristmill to Michael's former property that proved every bit as successful as the existing sawmill. Thomas ran the mills in Oriole until they were both destroyed by fire in 1869, and he retired at the age of sixty-five. Michael's return to Lansing would soon provide us with another beautiful farmhouse that survives to this day.

In 1859, Michael completed the red brick farmhouse that still stands near the eastern entrance to the York Cemetery. Much grander than his parents' frame house on Burndale Avenue, Michael's late Georgian style farmhouse owes a stylistic debt to the house that his friend, David Gibson, had built just around the corner at today's Yonge and Park Home Avenue, after he too was pardoned and allowed to return to North York. Thought by some to be a little *too* nice for a farmer at the time, Michael's house outlived the raised eyebrows and graces us still with its beauty. Michael lived and farmed on this lot that reached all the way from Yonge Street to Bathurst Street until his death in 1876.

Photo by Scott Kennedy

Michael Shepard's late-Georgian-style house, which was built in 1859 with a three-bay façade, appears as a small-scale version of David Gibson's five-bay Georgian house built several years earlier, and still standing less than a quarter of a mile north of Michael's house. The house is shown here as it looked on November 20, 2009.

After Michael's death, the farm remained intact until 1916 when the land was purchased by the Toronto General Burying Grounds as the site of a future cemetery. Michael's house, still in fine shape, was used as a private residence until the York Cemetery opened in 1948, at which time the house assumed the dual role of cemetery office and living quarters for the cemetery manager. Although now strictly given over to office space and the pallid, near-invisible throb of fluorescent lights, Michael Shepard's house still offers clear evidence of the enormous success of this family.

The year after Michael moved into his new farmhouse, his brother Joseph created one of the most memorable buildings in the history of North York. The combination store and living quarters he built on the northwest corner of Yonge and Sheppard would stand there for nearly 140 years as a landmark and lifeline for generations of North York families. The two-storey brick building with attic and full basement was constructed in the late Georgian style of the day, meaning simply that it exhibited the simplicity and symmetry consistent with Georgian architecture, augmented by a few details and flourishes of the neo-classical or Greek style. The building has no ninety-degree corners. It is, in fact, trapezoidal rather than square or rectangular, a situation that likely drove more than one of the bricklayers or carpenters across the street to the Golden Lion Tavern. There was a very practical reason for this somewhat bizarre construction, as shall be seen. The red and yellow bricks were said to have been hauled up from Yorkville by oxen. The wood used in the construction was produced at the Shepards' own sawmills.

Though commonly thought of as just a store, the building actually housed commodious living quarters as well. The store occupied the southeast corner of the building. It was a big store, graced with the usual pot-bellied stove in the centre, surrounded by long counters of dry goods on one side and foodstuffs on the other. The dry goods section featured bolts of cotton, flannel, woollens, denim, calico, and gingham. There were few ready-made clothes available in North York at the time, although such items as hats, gloves, and handkerchiefs were part of the store's regular stock.

The dry goods section also included a dizzying array of hardware, including tools, farm implements, saws, harnesses, rope, axes, nails, gunpowder, candles, kerosene lamps, and crockery. The food counters tempted customers with drawers full of salt, tea, oats, flour, coffee, dry mustard, chocolate, and sugar. Barrels of pickles and crackers complimented enormous, one-hundred-pound wheels of cheese just waiting to be cut to order. The barter system was still a normal way for farmers to exchange their products for the manufactured goods that they needed. This allowed the store to stock farm-fresh items such as butter, milk, eggs, fruits, and vegetables. The store kept long hours, from 7:00 a.m. to 10:00 p.m., Monday to Saturday. In addition, a wagon was loaded up once a week to make deliveries to farmers who were unable to do their buying in person.

The residential accommodations were equally impressive. To the north of the store, on the main floor, were the parlour and dining room, with a huge kitchen to the rear. At the very back was the summer kitchen, where meals could be prepared in warm weather without heating up the rest of the house. Temperature extremes were a fact of life then as now, and while the summer kitchen did an admirable job of keeping the place cooler in summer, the six large bedrooms on the second floor were always cold in winter, to the point that a glass of water carried up at bedtime would be frozen solid by morning. There was no central heating of any kind — no indoor plumbing and no electricity.

A deep well out back provided water for drinking and cooking, while a soft-water pump made bathing a little more pleasant. Also located to the rear of the house was a drive shed where the sleigh, buggy, and wagons were stored, as well as a barn with horse stalls, feed bins, tools, and a hay mow that offered endless hours of amusement for the children. To the north of the store stood the busy wagon and carriage shop of Cornelius van Nostrand III, whose family had been among the first pioneer farmers in York Mills, directly to the south. In later years, the wagon works would become the first home of the R.S. Kane Funeral Home, still serving the community today on Yonge Street, just south of Steeles Avenue.

The Shepard store was built as a trapezoid so it would fit exactly into the intersection, which was not square. The importance of this shape becomes clear when it is noted that the exterior of the store was as useful to the community as the interior. Shortly after the building was completed, a porch was added that offered shelter on the east and south sides of the building. The porch was built to shelter passengers who boarded stagecoaches and later, radial cars and buses on Yonge Street. The combination of the porch and the precise fit of the building to the intersection served to keep customers dry in bad weather, an important consideration since the store also functioned as a waiting room and ticket agent for the various types of transport down through the years. Local dairy farmers also used the porch when shipping pails of their milk. They would drop them off in the morning to be conveyed into the city for sale, then pick up the empty pails in the afternoon, or in the case of the early days of the stagecoaches, whenever they could make it back through the treacherous depths of Hogg's Hollow.

In 1866, the Shepards added another feature to the store when they were granted the rights to operate a post office. The name Lansing was suggested by Joseph's daughter, Saida, and was soon adopted by the entire area around the crossroads. The store was popular from the outset and before long it was the focal point of the community. In 1870, Joseph E. Shepard (Joseph III) took over the operation of the store from his father. He also assumed responsibility for the operation of the family's mills over by Bathurst Street, making his father, who had been born in 1815, an early exponent of "freedom fifty-five." Joseph Shepard II had many good years of retirement to look forward to, although one wonders if men like Joseph ever really retired. He died on April 24, 1899, at the age of eighty-four.

In 1888, Benjamin Brown took over the operation of the store on a rental basis. He changed the business from a general store to a hardware store to better serve the needs of the rapidly growing community. It was a prescient move. The store would remain a successful hardware store for the next 101 years. In 1899, Mary Jane Shepard, daughter of Joseph Shepard II, acquired the property for "$1.00 and natural love and affection," according to the deed, clearly a close family. In 1904, Benjamin Brown bought the property from Mary Jane and enlarged the former van Nostrand facilities to the north where a 1914 Model T Ford would soon be parked alongside the buggies, cutters, and wagons. In 1923, Benjamin sold the property to George and William Dempsey, whose family name would become as familiar to several generations of North Yorkers as the name Shepard.

By now the building had been modernized with the addition of indoor plumbing, central heating, and electricity. The Dempsey brothers, plumbers by trade, renamed the store the Dempsey Brothers' Hardware Store. In the 1930s, the second floor was extensively renovated to create two separate apartments for George and William's families. Dormer windows were added to the attic around the same time and the attic converted to a communal rec room that could be accessed from either of the apartments below.

In the 1960s, the store was taken over by George's sons, Bob and Jim. By the time they took over, the store had some local competition from such upstarts as the Kitchen family's Lansing Building Supply at Willowdale and Sheppard Avenues, and York Mills Hardware, operated by Msrs. Bannister and Jenkins at the corner of Bayview and York Mills. Nonetheless, Dempseys' remained *the* place to go for your hardware needs. Likely everyone living in North York back then has a Dempsey Brothers story or two.

In the 1950s and 1960s, a Saturday morning trip to Dempseys' was like a ritual. Many of the Second World War vets who now populated the area were pretty handy with a hammer and saw and much of the interior finishing work on

Photo by Ted Chirnside, Toronto Public Library, TC 24.

The Shepard/Dempsey store as it looked in 1955. The car in front of the store is a 1939 Ford. The car to the right appears to be a 1953 Oldsmobile.

the post-war houses that were covering the farms of North York was done by the owners. If the job was too complex for one person, neighbours could always be counted on to lend a hand, much like the barn-raisings of a not-too-distant past. Whether the job called for ten thousand nails or just one, Dempseys' could help, and the staff all knew just what kind of nail would do the job. The floors sagged and creaked underfoot. The bins behind the counter groaned under the weight of a seemingly endless array of screws, nails, nuts, bolts, and washers. Anything that might fall under the heading of "hardware" was in there somewhere. Maybe it was hanging from the ceiling or in a little drawer behind the counter or out back with the bags of fertilizer and cement or stashed upstairs or hidden in the basement, but if anyone in the whole city had it, it was probably the Dempsey brothers. Bob Dempsey liked to joke that he could fill a customer's order before the customer could get his wallet onto the counter.

By the end of the 1980s, the next mutation of North York was well underway. Mayor Mel Lastman's dream of a new downtown took root, as the high-rise wind tunnel endured today blew down precious history and replaced it with what many perceive to be an ill-conceived attempt to be something North York never was. In 1989, the Dempsey Brothers' Hardware Store was sold to the Canderel Development Corporation and the Prudential Assurance Company Limited. The new owners thought so much of their new acquisition that they turned it into a dollar store. A visit to the new store only emphasized the soullessness of the place. In place of the complex inventory of sturdy, essential items was a haphazard array of flimsy imported trinkets. In place of a caring, knowledgeable staff were bored, dismissive, and detached clock-watchers. The indignity continued for several years until the developers, finally devoid of ideas, gave the place to North York to avoid the cost of tearing it down.

North York wasted little time in devising a rescue strategy and soon a plan was in place that would see the old store moved out of harm's way. Building-moving specialists Charles Matthews Limited stabilized the structure and prepared for the half-mile move to the store's new home in a little park at the north end of Beecroft Road. On February 18, 1996, hundreds of people gathered in bone-chilling weather to witness a 463-ton building lifted off its foundations and driven down Beecroft Road. Supported by 128 wheels on nineteen dollies, the store began its laborious journey, taking nearly twelve hours to travel the half-mile distance. Once at the new location, the building was carefully placed on its new foundation.

The building was then restored under the supervision of the architectural firm Philip Goldsmith and Company Limited. The exterior of the building was restored to appear as it was in the Shepards' time. This meant the removal of the third-floor dormer windows and the re-creation of the original porch. The interior was completely re-imagined to serve an altogether new purpose as the new home of the North York Archives. Students, researchers, and members of the general public all looked forward to utilizing this precious resource. The architects were particularly proud of their accomplishment. A special publication called "The Dempsey Archivist" was published by the *North York Mirror* on Saturday, September 13, 1997, to mark the opening of the new archives. In it, architect Philip Goldsmith said:

> Archives and archive storage facilities generally are the toughest uses to put into a historic building. Archives, by their very nature, are for the long term storage of fragile material. We needed to create the maximum storage capacity in our work. We created a separate zone in the basement that was column free and high enough to maximize storage. In essence, we created a small building in a building. Also, we designed and incorporated our own vapour-barrier system to contain and control the humidity factor primarily in this space.

All in all, it was an expensive and time-consuming task that was extremely well done. Then something went terribly wrong.

In 1998, the provincial government, under then-premier Mike Harris, shocked the citizens of North York, East York, Scarborough, Etobicoke, York, and the City of Toronto by forcibly amalgamating these six separate entities into one unmanageable blob under the banner of "Toronto," despite the fact that an overwhelming majority of residents had voted against the amalgamation. The subsequent years have proven the residents right and the premier wrong as infrastructure and services have deteriorated to the point where few citizens ever expect to see a return to the modest efficiencies of pre-amalgamation. The casualties could fill a separate book, but the one that concerns us here is the fate of the North York Archives. On January 1, 1998, North York ceased to exist. It was now just a corner of Toronto. Shortly after, the archives that had been so proudly installed in the newly-renovated Shepard store were removed and amalgamated — some say "dumped," into the Toronto Archives on Spadina Road. The Shepards' store was abandoned once again.

Today, the building is home to the Beecroft Education Centre, named after Beecroft Road, where it now stands. The doors are all locked and there isn't so much as a plaque to tell passers-by this incredible story that embraces 150 years of our history. The northwest corner of Yonge and Sheppard was finally built upon in 2012, over fifteen years after the store was rolled away. It is now home to a 7-Eleven and a McDonald's. Perhaps that is all we need to know about the current state of land-use planning and respect for Canadian history in the new city of Toronto — but what about that extra "p" in Sheppard Avenue?

It seems that there was another family in Lansing at the time, known as "Sheppard," "Shepherd," and "Shephard." Record-keeping and literacy were a little rough-hewn in those days and such discrepancies were by no means uncommon. Most sources use "Sheppard" for the "other" family, as shown here. No one knows for sure which family the avenue was named after, and the prevailing opinion seems to be that it could be either/or.

In 1824, Thomas Sheppard bought the eastern 150 acres of Lot 15-1W, on the southwest corner of today's Yonge and Sheppard. That same year he built the Golden Lion Hotel, also referred to as the Golden Lion Inn, right on the southwest corner of the intersection. The Golden Lion was a large, square, two-storey frame structure with covered verandahs on both floors. There were large stables and barns to the south of the hotel and drive sheds to the north that could accommodate a dozen horses and horse-drawn vehicles. Upstairs were accommodations for twenty guests. Downstairs was a mud-brick kitchen at the back, and a tavern on the main floor. Thomas Sheppard's brother, Paul, was a noted wood carver, who carved the wooden spires of St. Paul's Anglican Church in L'Amoreaux (at the corner of Warden and Finch Avenues in Scarborough) and the original St. James's in the town of York. He created a spectacular mascot for his brother's new hotel when he carved a life-sized lion from a single pine stump.

The golden-coloured lion seemed to have a mind of its own, since some pictures show it on the second-floor balcony while others show it on the main floor, outside the front door. After many years of loyal service, it was replaced by another golden lion carved by Paul Sheppard around 1840, this time from oak with a flowing mane sculpted in plaster. (Dates given for this second statue range from 1833 to 1845.) The Golden Lion Hotel was an extremely important part of the community, hosting all sorts of events, from political meetings to dances, where Thomas and his sons, all accomplished musicians, provided the music in a dance hall that was built over the drive sheds. The dances would attract people from as far away as the town of York, some eight miles to the south, when a trip of that distance could have taken the better part of a day. Travellers of all stripes made frequent use of the Golden Lion and the other hotels up and down Yonge Street as a welcome respite from the gruelling road conditions. A common lament sung by farmers of the day went something like this:

"Here I am
On my way to Zion
I find my sons
In the Golden Lion."[3]

RESIDENCE OF REV. PICKETT.
LANSING. ONT.

The Golden Lion Hotel as it appeared in the early 1900s, with the second Golden Lion statue guarding the front door.

Photographer unknown, North York Historical Society, NYHS, 1080.

Thomas retired as proprietor in 1851. A John Meek took over as proprietor and ran the hotel until Thomas Sheppard's death in 1857. Thomas's son Charles inherited the farm and ran the hotel until 1869, at which point his sister Fanny and her husband, Cornelius van Nostrand II, took the hotel over and served as proprietors until 1870. That was the year that Charles sold the farm and hotel, keeping only the house he had built on present-day Sheppard Avenue in 1865.

In 1875, Charles sold the house to Mrs. Ann Carruthers. The storey-and-a-half clapboard house with the lovely barge-board trim stood at 25 Sheppard Avenue West — a familiar and welcome sight to local residents making their way home on the TTC, since the house stood directly opposite the bus terminal where it offered a tantalizing glimpse into our past until it was destroyed by fire in 1988.

The Golden Lion Hotel continued to operate into the early

twentieth century when it was purchased by the Reverend Thomas Webster Pickett and converted to a residence. The reverend converted the tavern into a meeting room where a Methodist Sunday School would meet and the roots of the Lansing United Church took hold. In 1902, the reverend's daughter, Anna-Keitha, married George S. Henry of Oriole Lodge Farm near Leslie and Sheppard. After the Picketts left the building, it served as the first municipal offices for the new municipality of North York, which was created in 1922. Six years later, the venerable old building was dismantled. Anna was given the golden lion, which lived on the verandah of Oriole Lodge until it was donated to the Sharon Temple Museum, just north of Newmarket, in 1953.

When the North York Historical Society was formed in 1960, the lion was returned to North York and can currently be found prowling the sixth floor of the North York Public Library.

CHAPTER TWO

The McBride Family Farms

A DRIVE NORTH ON BAYVIEW AVENUE WARRANTS A GLANCE AT the last house on the right, before arriving at Finch. It *looks* like an old house to be sure, but in these days of smoke and mirrors, appearances can sometimes be deceiving. Not here, however. Not this house — this house is over 150 years old, older than Canada itself, and built by a family who came to Upper Canada nearly 220 years ago. The McBrides were part of the very first wave of settlement in Upper Canada and they constructed a home that remains a private dwelling, well into the twenty-first century. The McBride family actually "bookend" the entire scope of European settlement in Upper Canada right up to the present day — defining them as a family with very few peers.

The house didn't always stand on Bayview. It was moved there in the 1970s, from its original location to the southeast, to save it from demolition when Burbank Drive was extended north of Burleigh Heights Drive. A debt of gratitude is owed to the people who saved this house and also to those who have maintained it for the last forty years, for they have preserved a priceless piece of our heritage and tangible evidence of this family's amazing journey.

Patriarch John McBride, his wife Hannah, and other family members left Ireland in the 1770s, bound for North America. They settled in Pennsylvania, a state often referred to as "a cradle of freedom," but one that probably wasn't the best choice for immigrants with Loyalist tendencies. When the American Revolutionary War broke out, the McBrides predictably fought with the British troops against the revolutionaries.

Little historical evidence exists to detail their efforts but the end result would become a common experience. Defeated Loyalists were clearly not welcome in the post-revolutionary United States of America, and, though many chose to move north of the border where they were welcomed with open arms, the McBrides returned to Ireland. There, John McBride was approached by John Graves Simcoe, his commander in the Revolutionary War, who had just been appointed the first lieutenant governor of Upper Canada. Simcoe enlisted him as a sergeant in the Queen's Rangers and enticed him to emigrate to Upper Canada with the promise of generous land grants. John McBride would not be disappointed and he would not disappoint.

Photo by Scott Kennedy

This house, built by David McBride in 1860, still stands on Bayview Avenue, where it was moved in the 1970s. Photo dated January 2013.

Upon arriving in Upper Canada in 1796, John was granted six hundred acres near the corner of present-day Bathurst and Lawrence, encompassing Lot 4-2W, Lot 5-2W, and Lot 4-3W, making him only the third landowner in what is now Downsview. Sergeant McBride, like many other military officers who received land grants, did not immediately set to clearing and fencing his land as required by Crown regulations. Rather, he served his adopted land in a more practical fashion by working with the Queen's Rangers to clear the forest from the area that is now downtown Toronto, where he had also been granted a small lot on King Street. If the concept of virgin forest in the downtown core seems hard to grasp, just remember that there were less than three hundred people living in the town of York when the McBrides arrived. In addition to his duties as a Queen's Ranger, John found it necessary to supplement his income in other ways and, once more, he and Hannah proved up to the task.

John and Hannah found employment almost immediately. He worked as a doorkeeper for both the Executive and Legislative Councils in the town of York, and, together with Hannah, provided catering services for the House of Assembly — a full workload indeed.

John died in 1801. It seems unlikely that he even had the chance to clear his land in Downsview. As was the reality of life then, early settlers didn't have the luxury of taking time to grieve; they just kept their heads down, kept their faith, and depended on hard work and family to get them through the dark hours. After John was gone, Hannah used her catering skills to open a tavern. Thankfully, the tavern was a great success as many members of the Legislature respected the McBrides and became regular customers.

Hannah sold Lot 4-3W in Downsview in 1803. Records do not indicate whether the Crown's requirements had been met, but rules were broken, of course. In this case, it seems possible that the Crown may have taken Hannah's situation into consideration and allowed the sale on compassionate grounds. The family's close relationship with Simcoe is some indication of how well-connected they were. Alternately, she may have paid someone else to do the work after John's death. The remaining two Downsview lots were willed to son Hugh McBride, who sold them by 1829.

Son John McBride II was the next to be the recipient of a Crown land grant. In 1830, he was granted Lot 17-1E, a 195-acre lot, which runs from Yonge Street over to Bayview Avenue, a quarter-of-a-mile north of Sheppard Avenue.

John II and his wife Eleanor had actually moved to this area sometime around 1806, buying fifteen acres of Lot 16-1E in 1814 and an additional forty-two acres of the lot in 1817. They were apparently not the most peaceful of settlers. In fact, they were summoned by the court to answer a charge of assault and battery brought by their neighbour Jacob Kummer (later Cummer), shortly after they had arrived. John McBride II was found innocent, but Eleanor was put on probation for a year and fined for her part in the misadventure. Members of the McBride family also competed in sanctioned fights, including the War of 1812, where they repaid the Crown's generosity by laying their lives on the line for their new home. This time, at least, they were on the winning side.

Following the War of 1812, John travelled to Ireland on a government-sponsored mission to recruit new settlers for Upper Canada. He was in Ireland for over a year, in the company of three First Nations friends who were also part of the mission. By all accounts, their trip was a great success and resulted in many enthusiastic Irish settlers immigrating to Upper Canada. Still, the venture was overshadowed, in the minds of many, by the accomplishments of John McBride's horses.

It seems that John and his three travelling companions had to drive a horse-drawn farm wagon from North York to New York City to book passage on a ship sailing for Ireland. Realizing that they would be gone for a long and undetermined length of time, John sold his two horses in New York before setting sail. Imagine John's surprise then, when he returned to his farm near Yonge and Sheppard over a year later to find the team of horses waiting for him. They had broken free from their new owner in Manhattan and found their way home — all the way to Willowdale.[1] Manhattan is an island. Never underestimate the power of your fellow animals.

Photo by Patricia Hart, North York Historical Society, NYHS 905.

Above: John McBride II's farmhouse was moved from his original 1830 land grant to sit next to its more modern neighbours on Spring Garden Road, as shown here in 1964.

Right: Townhouses now cover the spot where this house stood on Leslie Street until 1970, on the former farmland of John McBride III.

Photo by Dorothy Milne, North York Historical Society, NYHS 849.

John McBride III (1806–65) was born right around the time his parents moved to their farm on Yonge Street. By the time he was in his mid-twenties, however, the soil on the farm had become so light that when John III planted his potatoes, the wind would blow the topsoil right off the tops of the mounds. This was likely a result of the excessive removal of trees, the roots of which would normally anchor the soil. His solution was to buy the farm directly to the east on Lot 17-2E, which reached from Bayview east to Leslie and included the original site of the farmhouse that would be built by his son David in 1860. The house still stands on Bayview. John III built a house on the east edge of the lot, now on Leslie Street.

By all accounts, John III was a thrifty and industrious farmer. He also had a good head for business. When he died in 1865, he held the deeds to several different farms. He also gained some neighbourly brownie points when he joined Jacob Cummer's Wesleyan Methodist Church, doing his part to erase the memory of that little dust-up between his parents and Jacob that had occurred around the time he was born.

Two of John's sons also figure prominently in our history. Son Charles, born in 1832, clearly inherited his father's business acumen. In 1858, he bought the second Montgomery's Tavern, near today's Yonge and Eglinton. The first tavern on this site, built by John Montgomery in the early 1830s, had been the site of the skirmish that ended the Upper Canada Rebellion, and was burned to the ground by government troops on the night of December 7, 1837. When John Montgomery was pardoned some years later, he returned to the site and built a new tavern in 1843. After a while, John rented the tavern to his son William and opened two more taverns in the city of Toronto to the south.

When Charles McBride bought the rebuilt tavern, he renamed it Prospect House. Other than one year, from 1863–64, when the tavern was rented to a John Miller, Charles was the proprietor until 1870. In addition to functioning as a tavern and hotel, the structure also housed the York Township Council until 1871. In 1870, Charles sold the tavern to Thomas Beatty of Leslieville, who then sold it to one William Smith in 1873. It was William's misfortune to still be the owner when the tavern was destroyed by fire on November 20, 1881.

It seems that Charles still had the hospitality business in his veins. In 1873, he bought the Finch Hotel from John Finch who had built his inn on the northeast corner of present-day Yonge and Finch in 1847. Charles dismantled the hotel and rebuilt it on his fifty-acre farm on the west side of Yonge Street, just south of today's Fairlawn Avenue. The Bedford Park Hotel, as Charles renamed it, stood behind later storefront additions until the 1980s. In addition to his farming and inn-keeping, Charles also held the unpopular position of gate keeper at the Hogg's Hollow toll gate from 1878–80.

In 1860, Charles McBride's brother, David, built the house that stands today at 3167 Bayview Avenue. He was married to Angeline Mulholland, whose parents, Henry and Jane, had originally settled at today's Leslie and Sheppard, before moving to the Bathurst and Lawrence area where they were neighbours of John and Hannah McBride. David McBride met one of the saddest and most bizarre ends imaginable. It seems that David and Angeline were walking along the shore of the East Don River on July 14, 1877, on their way to visit her brother William on his farm at present-day Leslie and Sheppard, when David lost his footing. He slipped, hit his head, and fell, unconscious, into the water where, despite Angeline's best efforts to save him, he died.

The house that David built would continue to be home to subsequent generations of McBrides for nearly one hundred years after David's untimely death — a commendable legacy. The fate of the other McBride houses is not something that would inspire pride.

John McBride III's house was demolished around 1970 for a rather non-descript cluster of townhouses. John McBride II's second house, which had replaced the family's original log cabin on Lot 17-1E around 1875, was moved from its original location at Yonge and Empress to 43 Spring Garden Road in the 1920s. It remained there as

Photo by A.W. Galbraith, dated 1912. Toronto Public Library TC 5004.

Open farmland and towering elm trees stretch all the way to Bayview Avenue from behind Sarah and Robert McBride's house at 5043 Yonge Street.

a single-family dwelling until the early 1980s when all of the houses on this part of Spring Garden were purchased by developers Bramalea Limited, who intended to build a twenty-three-storey condominium on the property.

Plans that Bramalea submitted to the North York Planning Department in September 1981 called for the demolition of the house. The house was abandoned and the main floor was boarded up to deter local vandals, who retaliated by smashing the second-floor windows. In spite of such indignities, the house remained in fine overall condition and serious attempts were made to save it. Even the developers came on board and offered to pay the estimated cost of $45,000 of moving the house to another location. Bickering local politicians seemed unable to agree on any type of rescue plan, however, and another irreplaceable piece of Upper Canada's history was lost. A recent visit to the site, 43 Spring Garden Road, all commercial and industrial now, only served to re-emphasize the depressing result — not recommended for a viewing excursion.

Another McBride house, built on the same lot at a slightly later date, was the first brick house on this part of Yonge Street. In the early 1900s, it was the residence of Robert and Sarah McBride. By the early 1960s it was the residence and office of Dr. Ralph Johns. The house stood at 5043 Yonge Street, on the east side, just south of Hillcrest Avenue. Today, the site is occupied by the now-shuttered De Boers furniture store, sitting there awaiting redevelopment.

CHAPTER THREE

Elihu and Katherine Pease

STRANGELY ENOUGH, ELIHU PEASE'S FARMHOUSE WASN'T THE only one from the early farms of Willowdale that got cut in half. It is, however, the only one that was then transported to *three* different locations.

Elihu's ancestors emigrated from England aboard the Puritan ship *Francis*, landing in Boston in 1634. Elihu was born and educated in the United States. When he came to York in the early 1800s, he was a civil engineer and a land surveyor, so naturally he took a job as a schoolteacher. This may not be as bizarre as it seems, as in the early days it was mostly men who were schoolteachers, and teachers needed no real qualifications. In fact, they were often from the ranks of those who had already failed at numerous other pursuits, or suffered some physical impairment preventing them from taking on more rigorous work. Educated non-failures like Elihu were therefore highly prized. When he began teaching in the community of Langstaff in 1811, he was employed at the first school in York Township. His career as a teacher would be brief, however, and he was soon obliged to turn his back on the great pay — twenty-five cents per pupil, per month — and the glamorous living arrangements — billeted with a different student's family every two or three days.

As an American, Elihu refused to take the oath of allegiance to the British Crown when the War of 1812 was declared. Instead, he moved to Buffalo where he worked in the customs house and post office as well as running a tannery there for Jesse Ketchum, a tanner, and ultimately an astute businessman and politician with land just south of Yonge Street and Lawrence Avenue.[1] After the war, Elihu returned to York, swore his allegiance, and assisted in the rebuilding of the post-war town.

In 1819, Elihu married Jacob Cummer's daughter, Katherine, and moved to the hamlet of Newtonbrook on Yonge Street, between Finch and Steeles Avenues. He began farming Lot 23-1E, on the north side of today's Cummer Avenue, between Yonge Street and Bayview, and was once again teaching school. The family lived in the house on Yonge Street during this time, before selling their farm to Jacob Cummer and returning to Buffalo in 1821. Four years later, in 1825, they came home to North York for good and bought the southern half of their farm back from Jacob. At this point, Elihu once again returned to teaching as well as running his own farm and helping with his father-in-law's farm.

Elihu Pease and his wife, the former Katherine Cummer, lived for a time in this massive house that would later be home to other members of the Cummer family. It was built by a previous owner in 1819, the year the Peases were married, and stood at 6059 Yonge Street, across from today's Patricia Avenue until it was dismantled in 1964, the year this photograph was taken by Ted Chirnside.

Courtesy of Toronto Public Library, TC 115.

In 1834, the Peases would make their final move to the southeast corner of present-day Yonge and Sheppard, where they bought the northwest eighty-six acres of the 190-acre farm on Lot 15-1E that had been granted to constable and tavern-owner John Everson in 1803. Elihu built a small tannery on his new farm and, as if farming and tanning weren't enough to keep him busy, he became interested in politics. He was elected pathmaster for the county of York in 1836, clerk of York Township in 1837, and would later be appointed inspector of schools. In 1844, the year that the new brick St. John's Anglican Church was opened, Elihu bought the old log church and moved it to his farm where he re-assembled it to serve as a shed.

Elihu's son Edward was apprenticed to his father as a tanner, eventually opening his own tannery in today's King Township on land donated by his father. Elihu's daughter Elizabeth married another tanner, Andrew Davis. Andrew's

Photo by Scott Kennedy

The front half of Elihu Pease's house is shown at its current location on Harrison Garden Boulevard. It was moved there in 2002.

father James ran a large inn on the southwest corner of Yonge and Finch, and had also opened a small tannery there in 1834. When Andrew was learning the trade he made frequent visits to the Pease tannery, inspired no doubt by the opportunity to spend some time with Elizabeth. For love to bloom in a tannery, it must have been true.

Elihu Pease died in 1854 and all of his property was auctioned off, right down to his tools, boots, and shoes. The effects of Andrew Davis's tannery were disposed of in the same auction, but since the Davis family leather business continued well into the twentieth century, it would appear that this auction was part of a greater plan. The next two generations of the

Davis family would both count an "Elihu" Davis among their numbers. And what of Elihu Pease's farmhouse, built in 1834 when he and Katherine first moved to Yonge and Sheppard? It's a complicated tale, but one worth telling.

The Pease family stayed on the farm until 1871. The 1861 census shows Elihu's son, Edward, and his wife, Sarah, as well as six dependents (possibly including nieces, nephews and/or servants' children) living on the farm. The census also lists the crops on the farm, including wheat, barley, peas, oats, potatoes, turnips, and carrots. In addition, the family was selling wool, cider, butter, beef, and pork. When the family moved to King Township in 1871, the farm was sold to the pioneer Harrison family of York Mills. In 1896, the Harrisons sold the farm, 110 acres, to Joseph Christie Bales, whose family had been farming in the area since 1819. One of the first things Joseph Bales did was to remodel the original Pease farmhouse. In 1921, the house was cut in half, with the front half being moved to 34 Avondale Avenue and the back half to 17 Bales Avenue. Joseph Christie Bales's farmhouse (see 1955 photo in the next chapter), was built on the former Pease property. Descendant Clarence Bales was the last family member to live in this house.

The rear half of Elihu's house that was moved to Bales Avenue was demolished some time ago. The front half that was relocated to Avondale Avenue in 1921 is fortunately still with us. In 2002, after a long struggle that involved the City of Toronto, the Ontario Municipal Board, the Avondale Ratepayers Association, the North York Historical Society, the developer, and the Badone family, who owned the house, it was decided to move the house around the corner to its current location on Harrison Garden Boulevard, a street named after another pioneer family.

Donalda and Louis Badone had been living in the Pease house for over forty years, and, though they had hoped to see it remain on Avondale Avenue, they were painfully aware that they were not going to get their wish. When the developer made it clear that demolition or relocation were the only options, a deal was struck whereby the developer was awarded an incentive density[2] that allowed him to generate the funds required to move the house around the corner and restore it to a semblance of the way it was in the late 1800s.

And there it sits on its little patch of grass, with a row of pine trees to keep it company, surrounded by high-rise condominiums. The outside has been restored as promised, with the original clapboard now painted the same shade of cream that was discovered under the brick facing, which had been added when the house was divided and moved in 1921. The inside of the house didn't fare so well. Last year it was turned into sales offices for the condominiums.

Chapter Four

The Bales Family Farms

Of all the pioneer families in North York, none was more politically active than the Bales family. By the fourth generation, family members had held the offices of school trustee, councillor, deputy reeve, and reeve; as well as Ontario MPP and provincial cabinet minister. It all began when John Bales of Cumberland and his wife, Elizabeth Scott, originally from Yorkshire, decided to leave England for the New World in 1819.

Shortly after their arrival in what became the Township of North York, John and Elizabeth purchased the western sixty acres of Lot 15-1W. Their farm occupied the southeast corner of present-day Bathurst and Sheppard. The eastern border of the farm was the massive valley of the West Don River. Their neighbours on the lot were John Sheppard, who owned the northeastern section, which reached all the way over to Yonge Street, and Andrew McGlashan, who owned the southeast corner of the lot, between Yonge Street and the river.

The house that the Bales' built on their farm in 1822 still stands today, and a good thing too, for the house is apparently one of only a few of its kind to ever be built in pioneer Ontario. The one-and-a-half-storey house is built of logs and covered in rough-cast concrete — a combination of mortar and small pebbles. The symmetrical plan and elevation of the house echo the style of the rural English cottages of the Bales's youth, and although this style and construction method are rare in Ontario, similar houses are quite common in New York State. A kitchen wing was added to the house sometime before 1850 to accommodate a growing family that would eventually include ten children. It goes without saying that the house was well built since it has already survived for nearly 190 years. The house still sits on its original site, which is now part of the north end of Earl Bales Park, not too far south of Sheppard Avenue. In 1833, John expanded the farm to 160 acres when he purchased one hundred acres of Lot 14-1W, directly to the south, the lot that had originally been granted to potter Thomas Humberstone in 1812.

In 1881, the farm was sold to the Grand Trunk Transportation Company, although no rail lines were ever laid anywhere near the farm. In fact, this part of Bathurst Street was long considered to be ill-suited to any type of travel owing to the extreme width and depth of the river valley.

John Bales's house, the first farmhouse that the family built in Upper Canada. Ironically, the only one of their homes still standing, is shown here in Earl Bales Park on February 19, 2010.

Maps from 1892 to 1910 show a stable period of ownership for the farms on the two lots, with George McCormack farming the northeast ninety acres of Lot 15-1W, which was formerly owned by John Sheppard, and the Shedden Company owning the Bales's 160 acres at Bathurst and Sheppard. The Shedden Company, also spelled "Sheddon" on

some documents, was formed in 1887 to operate flour mills in the area. As well as milling on the former Bales farm, the company also operated another mill a mile or so downriver in Hogg's Hollow until 1897.

The farms would exist until the 1950s when the acreage to the east of the river valley was subdivided for houses, and the

Photo by Scott Kennedy

Bales farm, to the west of the valley, became the York Downs Golf Club. The club continued as a part of the community, preserving a tremendous amount of green space until 1968, when the land was sold to the City of Toronto and the club moved to a new facility near the corner of Kennedy Road and Sixteenth Avenue in Markham. The former golf course was then transformed into the current Earl Bales Park and Earl Bales Ski and Snowboard Centre — the steep hills are still in use and were just upgraded with a million-dollar-plus ski lift, paid for by the City of Toronto. Remnants of the golf course's landscaping are still clearly visible on the park's tableland along Bathurst Street.

So who exactly *is* Earl Bales? His story will appear as part of that fourth generation of Bales (later in this chapter). Several of John and Elizabeth's children would marry and leave North York to farm elsewhere. Son Joseph, however, stayed put and started the branch of the family that would ensure the Bales name would not soon be forgotten.

In 1885, Joseph Bales bought a farm on Lot 15-1E from the Harrison family of York Mills. The northern border of the farm was Sheppard Avenue. It was bounded by Bayview Avenue to the east and Yonge Street to the west. The farm had previously been owned by members of other pioneer families, including Stillwell Willson, Jacob Cummer, Elihu Pease, and Christopher Harrison II. In 1888, Joseph bought the western half of Lot 14-1E directly to the south. He now had nearly three hundred acres of farmland at the corner of Yonge and Sheppard. In 1896, the land was passed on to his sons. Joseph Christie Bales settled on Lot 15-1E and his brother, Oliver Douglas Bales, settled on the western half of Lot 14-1E. Maps from 1910 show that the farms were still owned by the two brothers.

In the 1920s, Joseph and Oliver employed a family of gypsies to work on their farms. The gypsies were skilled blacksmiths who spent much of their time shoeing the Bales' horses.

On Sundays the little family would take their covered wagon, which contained all of their worldly goods, down to the river in Hogg's Hollow where they would do their laundry and hang it up to dry under the old bridge that once spanned the river just north of the Jolly Miller. The horses and dogs enjoyed a well-deserved dip in the cool water while the family bathed and swam before moving to the sand beach that once existed where the Miller's parking lot is today. There they would play games and enjoy a picnic lunch while their clothes dried in the summer breeze. When the shadows began to grow long they would pack up their wagon and trundle back up the hill to the Bales' farms.

Once common in Canada, the nomadic gypsies quietly disappeared or were assimilated into conventional society as the twentieth century progressed. One of the last remnants of their presence in North York was an abandoned gypsy wagon that survived into the 1960s, abandoned by a little creek,[1] now buried, that flowed parallel to Bannatyne Drive on the former Harrison farm in York Mills.

By the 1920s, parts of the Bales' farms were being sold for housing as the city pushed ever further northward. Initially, the sales were to individuals for construction of individual houses, but as the years progressed, the concept of the "subdivision" reared its inevitable head. This concept of simultaneous construction of massive numbers of houses in a given area would prove the death knell for all of the farms in North York, and yet the Bales' farms would survive a lot longer than most of their neighbours'.

Brothers Joseph Christie Bales and Oliver Douglas Bales belonged to the third generation of their family to farm in North York, but they were the first members of their family to become active in local politics. Oliver served on the first North York Council from 1922 to 1923, along with James Muirhead, William Scrace, W.J. Buchanan, and Reeve R.F. Hicks. Joseph Christie Bales would also serve on council in 1927.

Photographer unknown, The North York Historical Society, NYHS 1024.

Above: *The success of the Bales family farms is amply demonstrated by the style, size, and detail of Oliver Douglas Bales's farmhouse on Yonge Street, south of Sheppard; shown circa 1910.*

Left: *Later additions and renovations to the Bales farmhouse, such as the enclosed sunroom and wraparound porch, give further indication of the Bales family's continued success. The house is shown in 1959 on the corner of Yonge Street and the fledgling Highway 401, which had been built through this area four years earlier and was still only two uncrowded lanes in each direction.*

Photo by Ted Chirnside, Toronto Public Library, TC 268

The accompanying photos show Joseph Christie's house still standing at Yonge and Sheppard in 1955, and his brother's house and barn stubbornly ensconced at the corner of Yonge and the 401 in 1959. The former would not last long, and the latter farm, down to one acre when the photos were taken in 1959, would be sold by the family in 1960. As riveting as these photos are, it would be the accomplishments of two of the men who were born in these houses that would outshine the pioneer family's farming history. One of these men was the aforementioned Earl Bales, of Earl Bales Park fame.

Oliver Douglas Bales's twin sons, Earl and Allen, were born in 1896. Earl joined the army to serve in the field artillery in 1915. After returning from the First World War he married Ruth Bick. Together, they would raise two daughters, Barbara and Mary. In 1931, Earl followed in his father's footsteps when he was elected as a North York councillor. In 1933, he was elected deputy reeve and in 1934 became the youngest reeve in North York history at the age of thirty-eight. When he took over as reeve from George Elliot, whose farm is also featured in these pages, he landed squarely in the middle of the fiscal nightmare of the Great Depression.

In 1933, North York had defaulted on payments to its bond holders, a situation shared by virtually every other municipality in the province. In 1935, shortly after Earl had taken power, North York was put under provincial supervision by Queen's Park. This meant that any financial transactions made by North York would have to be approved by the provincial government. Under Earl's leadership, North York performed admirably, and, by the end of 1937, they had paid off all of their bond holders. Earl Bales would remain as reeve until 1940. In 1941, North York was released from the supervision of the provincial government, one of only a handful of municipalities in the entire province to have achieved this goal. During these years Earl was also a member of the York County Council.

After his days as an elected official were over, Earl Bales returned to private life for a while before finding a new home on the North York Planning Board. He served on the board for twenty-six years, from 1946 to 1972, and was the chairman for seventeen of those years. His tenure encompassed the greatest population boom in the history of North York. Earl was particularly well suited to this challenge, for despite his pioneer roots and farming background, he was overwhelmingly pro-development. When the fields, farms, and orchards of his youth began to be replaced by housing, he wasn't mournful or bitter. Rather, he embraced the change, and, in fact, facilitated the rapid urbanization by sanctioning new zoning bylaws, which allowed for the construction of highrise apartment buildings.

It seems that he viewed the loss of the farms as inevitable and wanted to retain some degree of control as to how the bulldozers rolled. In an interview with Sheila White, published in the *Willowdale Mirror* on January 9, 1985, Earl recalled that: "After World War II the boom started from the Humber River right over to Victoria Park Avenue. We wanted to create proper development which would be a benefit to North York, not a burden. We always looked forward to developing this area."

Earl would live out the latter part of his life in one of these new developments, at Bayview Village on the former Kingsdale Farm property, after selling and vacating the last acre of the family farm at Yonge Street and Highway 401 in 1960. True to his farm roots, he looked after his ravine property on Forest Grove Drive as long as his health would allow, continuing to take care of the gardening and snow shovelling until he was nearly ninety. He died there suddenly on July 31, 1992. He was ninety-five. His cousin and best friend, Dalton Bales, would climb even higher on the political ladder but would meet a much more bizarre and premature end.

Courtesy of Toronto Public Library, TC 24A.

The message of this book is aptly summarized in this 1955 photograph by Ted Chirnside. This is the corner of Yonge and Sheppard on a swelter-ing summer afternoon, as seen from beneath the protective overhang of the Dempsey Brothers' store. Looking to the southeast: from left to right, a new branch of the Bank of Toronto; Joseph Christie Bales's farmhouse, abandoned and soon to be demolished for a plaza; a billboard for the now-vanquished Simpson's department stores; and an honour box belonging to the Globe and Mail — *a photograph more eloquent than words.*

Photo by J.V. Salmon, Toronto Public Library, S 1-3149C.

The modern world takes over as the McLean-Hunter building, built on former Bales farmland in 1949, lurks behind the barn on Oliver Douglas Bales's farm on the northeast corner of Yonge Street and Highway 401 in 1959. The massive printing facility, one of North York's earliest industries, was demolished in 1995 for condominium towers.

Joseph Christie Bales's son Dalton was born in 1920. He grew up on his parents' farm at the corner of Yonge and Sheppard. After graduating from high school he decided to pursue a career in law. He eventually became a partner in the Toronto firm of McLaughlin, Soward, a firm he joined as a student in 1946. Three years later, he was called to the bar. His political career began in 1959 when he was elected to the North York Township council, where his father, uncle, and cousin Earl had served in previous decades. He would remain a councillor until 1962, in addition to serving as chairman of the North York Board of Health from 1960 to 1965, yet he had ambitions beyond the confines of municipal politics.

In 1963, Dalton was elected to the Ontario Legislature as the member from the riding of York Mills, a riding he would represent for twelve years. In 1966, he was appointed minister of labour by then-Premier John Robarts. He was later appointed provincial attorney general, a position he held from 1972 until 1974, while simultaneously serving as the minister of municipal affairs. He suffered a heart attack in 1974 and quit politics the following year, citing obvious concerns for his health. He then retired to his home near Bayview and York Mills.

On the evening of October 30, 1979, one night before Hallowe'en, Dalton Bales was attempting to cross Bayview Avenue about a block south of York Mills Road when he was struck and killed by a car in the northbound passing lane. He was fifty-nine.

So what remains as the family's legacy? Well, first of all, there is that magnificent park — one of the few places left in North York where you can still stand on open land where cattle once grazed and crops once grew. The existence of the park has also assured the survival of the family's original farmhouse and even parts of their barns, which now serve as maintenance sheds for park staff. The house is currently used as an Ontario Early Years Centre for parents and children.

The park is also home to the Earl Bales Community Centre, the Holocaust Education and Memorial Centre of Toronto and the previously mentioned ski centre. Other than that, there is not much left of the farms, except for the tiny Bales Avenue, a two-block road to nowhere, east of Yonge Street and south of Sheppard, which is currently little more than a shortcut for construction vehicles. Near the southern end of Bales Avenue, on Harrison Garden Boulevard, stands the front half of the Elihu Pease house that Joseph Christie Bales cut in half and moved to Avondale Avenue in 1921. The house was moved to its current location in 2002.

But it's the most obscure piece of the Bales' family legacy that may be the most charming. In 1921, when Joseph Christie Bales moved Elihu Pease's farmhouse from Yonge and Sheppard to make room for his own house, he also dismantled an old shed on the property that had once been the original St. John's Anglican Church, built in 1817, high on a hill overlooking Hogg's Hollow. When the current stone church was built on the site in 1844, Elihu bought the old church, dismantled it, and moved it to his farm, where it was rebuilt to serve as a shed. In 1921, the timbers of the former church/shed were stored in the Bales' barn, where they remained until 1948. That year, St. John's began building an addition that would include a new chancel and memorial chapel. When the Bales family heard of the new construction, they donated the timbers of the original wooden church to be used in the ceiling of the new chancel and chapel. The adze marks made by the men who squared these primeval timbers nearly two hundred years ago, are still clearly visible today

Chapter Five

The Risebroughs: Robert I, Robert II, Robert III, Roy, and William

When the Township of North York was created in 1922, it had a population of 6,000 and a police force of one. Roy Risebrough, fourth generation North York farmer, born on the family farm near today's Bayview and Cummer, was definitely his own boss. Not only was he the lone constable on a force of one, he was also the chief. It's not surprising that Roy would hold a position of prominence in the early days of North York, as it can be said without exaggeration that without Roy's efforts, there might not even *be* a North York.

Roy was one of five disgruntled farmers who crisscrossed the area in 1921 gathering signatures on a petition to secede from the Township of York. He was also one of the people charged with raising money to pay for the lawyer, who would be required to conduct the secession proceedings. As the urban population of Toronto grew, fewer and fewer farmers were being elected to York Township Council until, in 1919, for the first time, no farmers were elected at all. The farmers, who were paying nearly 25 percent of the township's taxes, decided that something had to be done. In 1921, James Muirhead, John Brumwell, W.J. Buchanan, and W.C. Snider piled into Roy Risebrough's Model T Ford and

visited all the farmers in the area to drum up support. Their efforts paid off quickly and in grand fashion. In 1922, the province granted their request and the Township of North York was born. Roy's contributions were significant as he was the only one of the five who had a car, which made reaching all the farmers that much easier.

The new council had its work cut out for it, as North York was on the cusp of an unprecedented growth spurt. By the time Roy retired as police chief in 1957, he would be dealing with over 182,000 residents, a far cry from the 6,000 he had to worry about in the beginning. And, yes, by 1957, he had plenty of help.

Roy was born on the farm where he would live his whole life. Located on the northeast fifty acres of Lot 22-1E, on the southwest corner of Bayview and Cummer, the farm had been in the family since 1862. Roy was born there thirty years later. Forty-five years after Roy's birth, the family farmhouse would gain a new neighbour when St. John's Convalescent Hospital opened on part of the Montgomery/Elliot farm in 1937, just to the west of the Risebroughs' farm

Roy studied at the little red-brick Newtonbrook Public School on Drewry Avenue before graduating from Richmond

Hill High School and the Ontario College of Agriculture in Guelph. He would spend the next six or seven winters inspecting dairy cattle throughout the province and farming in the summer. He married Ida Congram of Wingham and together they had two daughters.

At the time Roy was appointed chief of police in 1922, he was also given the posts of school attendance officer and sanitary inspector, and yet he continued to inspect dairy cattle in the winter and farm in the summer. The fact that he was able to wear so many hats says a lot about the relative lack of crime in North York in the 1920s. With automobiles still beyond the reach, or taste, of most North York residents, crime was much more localized than it is today. In addition, Roy was dealing mostly with people he knew on a personal level. After all, his family had been farming here for over eighty years by the time North York was created. Crime was often minor: the odd burglary, a little rustling, public drunkenness, and domestic disputes were the types of things that Roy was likely to encounter. He never wore a gun and only wore a uniform twice — on ceremonial occasions.

As the population grew, Roy was obliged to hire additional officers. John Harrison was perhaps the most significant of Roy's early hires. He joined the force in 1930, becoming deputy chief in 1946, and working in the community on such projects as the restoration of the Zion Primitive Methodist Church, usually going beyond the call of duty. The descendant of another pioneer family, John would become district chief when the North York force was absorbed by the Metropolitan Toronto Police in 1957. He is buried in the Zion Church cemetery that he helped to restore.

John Harrison wasn't the only addition to the force, which had grown to thirteen officers by 1944. The township population had grown to 25,000 by this point, but it would be the post-war years that would see a real explosion in both population and crime. By 1953 the population of North York had exploded to over 110,000. Crime grew as well, for now the area was well-serviced by hundreds of new roads and nearly everyone had access to a car. Bank robbers, in particular, took aim at the new, isolated suburban banks, which offered a more enticing choice of getaway routes than their downtown contemporaries. It was Roy's men who, in 1952, captured two members of the notorious Boyd gang[1] who had escaped from the Don Jail and were hiding out in an abandoned barn on the old Hildon Farm near Finch and Leslie.

The unfettered population growth and the corresponding expansion of the police force meant that the force seemed to be constantly looking for new police stations. In 1955, the twenty-nine member division that served Don Mills had to be housed in one of the barns at the former Don-Alda Farm, near the corner of Don Mills Road and York Mills Road. By 1957, the North York force had grown to two hundred officers. Through it all, Roy's influence continued to grow. He became somewhat of an elder statesman whose opinion was sought and valued by members of the community. His endorsement often meant the difference between victory and defeat for local politicians, in a time when it was considered perfectly normal for municipal employees to involve themselves in this way

Several months before the North York Police Force was absorbed into the new Metropolitan Toronto Police Force in 1957, Roy Risebrough retired. It seemed a perfect convergence of events for the former one-man show. He had reached retirement age that year and had certainly earned his leisure, but he was also able to neatly sidestep being rolled into the huge new bureaucracy, a near miss that probably pleased this rugged individual. He retired to the family farmhouse on Cummer, staying involved through local service groups, police associations, and the Newtonbrook United Church.

Photo by Lorne Gardner, North York Historical Society, NYHS 42.

In a time before graffiti, there was a certain elegance in abandonment, and a chance to explore and appreciate what once was, before it was defaced. The empty, haunted eyes of this massive Risebrough farmhouse, photographed on the south side of Cummer Avenue, just east of Bayview in 1961, beckon a visitor to enter an interior that would have offered the senses a visceral education to shame the most elaborate video game or surround-sound movie. It was demolished in the mid-1960s and high-rise apartment buildings took over the site.

Roy's ancestors did historians no favours by making sure that they were all named "Robert." His father, grandfather, great-grandfather, and brother all carried this handle with only the odd middle initial to differentiate them from one another. Robert I started it all when he left the county of Norfolk in England and sailed to Canada with his wife and six children in 1837. After a nightmarish thirteen weeks at sea they finally arrived

in Upper Canada, sick, tired, and hungry. One source indicates that they first farmed the northeast corner of Lot 22-1E, the section near Bayview and Cummer, but this is difficult to prove.

The land, which had previously been home to Alexander and John Montgomery, was owned by the Cummers when the Risebroughs arrived, so if they did start there it would have been as tenants. What *is* certain is the fact that Robert I bought the east quarter of Lot 21-3E on the northwest corner of Finch and Woodbine in 1852. It was not until 1862 that his name appeared on the deed to the northeast corner of the lot on Cummer. The same year he also bought the western half of Lot 22-2E on the southeast corner of Bayview and Cummer. When Robert I died in 1871, he left the farms to his son Robert II, who had been born in England in 1827 and survived that hellish Atlantic crossing at the age of ten. In 1891, Robert II bought the southwest corner of Lot 23-1W and expanded an existing farmhouse there on the northeast corner of Bathurst Street and Drewry Avenue.

In 1890, William Risebrough, one of Robert Risebrough II's sons, bought sixty acres of the seventy-five-acre Lot 22-4E, north of Finch on the east side of Woodbine. The remaining fifteen acres was part of the Myers family holdings. By 1891, the Risebroughs had a farm in every one of the four concessions east of Yonge Street, as well as one farm west of Yonge. They were also farming in Scarborough, to the east of Victoria Park Avenue.

As already seen with Roy, the family continued to farm until after the Second World War, when pressures from the growing city began to gobble up all of the remaining farmland in North York. But, the family's contribution to farming still wasn't over. Their more easterly farms, near Finch and Woodbine, continued as productive farmland until the 1960s. Post-war development generally flowed east and west from Yonge Street, and farms on the far eastern and western borders of North York were the last to be paved over.

In 1946, a small subdivision was created on the former Risebrough farm on the southwest corner of Bayview and Cummer, but this subdivision was different. Created and operated under the federal government's Veterans Land Act (VLA), the oversized one-half-acre lots were designed to allow returning veterans and their families enough space to grow their own food. The lots featured frontages that ranged from 110 feet to 140 feet.

One of 124 such communities in Canada, "Risebrough," as the new community was called, was an immediate hit with the fifty families lucky enough to live there. The going was rough at first but as the new settlers persevered they soon created a way of life that made all of their efforts worthwhile.

Like most subdivisions, this one started out as a sea of mud, but as the new residents landscaped and developed their properties, a very different scene began to emerge. By 1949, all fifty families had moved into their new homes and were beginning to see the first produce from their gardens. In a way, the new community was like a collection of mini farms, where neighbours still had a commonality of purpose. Large projects, such as the construction of garages or additions to the houses were accomplished by all of the residents coming together to pitch in, much as the farmers before them had depended on barn-raising bees and the like to realize their dreams. The growing of fruits and vegetables was undertaken in a serious way, to the point that most families were able to harvest enough produce in the fall to get them through the entire winter.

John MacKenzie, who had spent most of the Second World War on corvettes in the North Atlantic, is a case in point. "We grow almost every type of vegetable," he said, when quoted in *The Willowdale Enterprise* of October 20, 1949. "We put them in a cold storage bin in the basement and they last us all through the winter. Last spring we had enough potatoes left to cut up and plant for this year's crop."[2] The family only needed to buy butter, meat, and a few packaged items to get them through the winter. The MacKenzies won an award for having the best landscaped and developed VLA lot in Ontario. Although most of the veterans were employed in Toronto after the war, they couldn't wait to get home at night to their plots and garden tractors. Orchards planted by the families soon yielded peaches, pears, plums, cherries, and apples. Fall was the time for harvesting and ploughing.

Photo by Ted Chirnside, Toronto Public Library, TC 117.

Looking northwest across Bayview Avenue, just north of Finch. The William Ford farm can be seen in the foreground, and several of the houses in the little suburb of Risebrough in the background. The Fords began farming this eighty-acre parcel in 1886. Today, this would essentially be a photo of the Bayview Arena, but here, in 1955, a well-kept working farm and the garden plots of Risebrough continue to stand their ground.

The package of house and lot cost an average of $7,200, although the veterans were only required to pay $5,200 back to the government. Amortized over twenty-five years, the mortgage payments were approximately $19.00 per month for a bungalow and $25.75 for a six-room, storey-and-a-half house. The 3.5 percent interest rate was the only figure that would appear even remotely familiar to present-day residents. Property taxes, which had started out around $40.00 a year in 1946, had *soared* to $55.00 three years later. To put things in perspective though, it should be realized that this represents a 38 percent increase. Imagine the outcry if that kind of burden were imposed on today's property owners? It should also be remembered that a salary of $50.00 a week would have landed you squarely in the middle class during the immediate post-war years.

The MacKenzies weren't the only family in Risebrough to win an award. Their neighbours, the Yules and the Ives, also won in the category of Veterans Individual Small Holdings. The community itself was judged the best in its class, out of all 124 similar communities in Canada. The federal government had high hopes for this type of initiative. Milton Gregg, the federal minister in charge of veterans' affairs said, when he announced the competition in 1948, that "The small holding way of life has great potential for stabilizing our economy. It will command the interest of town planners in countries other than Canada."[3] Sadly, this noble little initiative was no match for the overwhelming influx of humanity that would wash over North York for the next three decades.

When the first vegetable gardens were planted in Risebrough, North York had less than forty thousand residents. Twenty-five years later there were more than *half-a-million* people occupying the same space. The lovely idea of a reasonable number of people sharing the land in such a way that they could grow some of their own food was sacrificed on the altar of unfettered growth. The promise of increased tax revenue, which always sets municipal politicians to salivating, may look good on paper, but it is never enough to cover the costs incurred by a massive population explosion. Where there was once a dream of self-sufficiency, there is now welfare and food banks. Where there was once one unarmed police officer, there now are thousands in bullet-proof vests. Where people once enjoyed a little fresh air and elbow room, today's citizens are now forced to endure smog alerts, gridlock, and road rage. If Roy had known it would come to this, he might have left the Model T in the barn.

Risebrough Avenue still exists to mark the place where a hopeful little subdivision was swallowed by a ravenous city, the frontages now divided two or three times over to cram in as many houses as possible. Seneca College occupies the Risebroughs' original farm at Finch and the Don Valley Parkway. The rest of their farms are now covered by houses, apartment buildings, and shopping centres. One Risebrough farmhouse still stands in Scarborough, on the east side of Victoria Park, halfway between Steeles and Finch. It currently houses a mosque, which almost certainly means that it will only stand until enough money is raised to build a *proper* mosque. All of the family's other farmhouses are gone, except for one, and what a neat little story that is.

In 1980, the farmhouse that Robert Risebrough II had bought at the corner of Bathurst and Drewry was slated for demolition, since the area was being re-developed. The exact build date of the house remains undocumented, although it is known that it was built on a ten-acre parcel of Lot 23-1W that had been severed from the lot in 1847. That was the year that Drewry Avenue was opened up from Yonge Street to Bathurst Street after William Durie bought the south half of the lot and subdivided it into smaller lots that ranged from five to thirty acres. The Risborough house started out as a simple frame worker's cottage that was possibly constructed by James Hale, who owned the ten-acre lot from 1851 to 1861, although any positive determination is purely speculative. It does seem clear, however, that "Drewry'" is a mutation of William Durie's surname.

William Durie was a retired English army officer when he came to Upper Canada in 1836. The thoroughfare that would ultimately bear a modified version of his name was initially known as "Pope's Lane," because of the preponderance of Roman Catholics who built houses there. The Risebrough house came into the family by way of the Wood family who had purchased the house in 1872. Six years later the house was owned by William Woods, who was Robert Risebrough II's father-in-law. Robert and family took the house over in 1891 and were probably the ones who added the second storey. The house would remain in the Risebrough family until the late 1970s, the final residents being Charles Risebrough and his wife, Janet (McCorkell) Risebrough. By the time Charles died, on August 19, 1978, the house was surrounded by new development and stood on the last undeveloped corner in the area.

One day in 1980, while the vacant farmhouse waited for the bulldozers, it caught the eye of Bob Holland, who was then the head of the Industrial Arts Department at nearby R.J. Lang Junior High School. Bob immediately saw a tremendous opportunity to save a part of our history and give his students some real-world experience at the same time. In a scene that is not likely to repeat itself today, Bob convinced the developer to allow his students to carefully dismantle the house so it could be rebuilt and preserved at another location. The developer agreed and the North York Board of Education offered up their outdoor education centre near Bolton as a site for the reconstruction. The R.J. Lang students carefully dismantled the house, numbering each piece of wood to facilitate re-assembly. The pieces were then moved to the outdoor education centre, but before they could be put back together, the North York Board of Education closed R.J. Lang Junior High at the end of the school year in 1982.

The project didn't find its legs again until 1983, when Bob Holland took over the Industrial Arts Department of Windfields Junior High, built in 1970 on one of the last remnants of E.P. Taylor's Winfields Farm, where Northern Dancer once frolicked near the corner of York Mills Road and Leslie Street. Twenty lucky Windfields students then took up where their counterparts at R.J. Lang left off and, under the supervision of Bob Holland, reconstructed the Risebrough farmhouse on its new site to serve as a teaching facility for those interested in learning about a vanquished way of life.

Mr. Holland deserves our thanks. Though not a work of literature or musical composition, this project must certainly be considered an opus.

CHAPTER SIX

Barberry Place: The Thomas Clark Farm Lot

THOMAS CLARK BUILT BARBERRY PLACE IN 1855 TO HOUSE his growing family, which would eventually include thirteen children. The prolific Mr. Clark had purchased his property in 1841, the two-hundred-acre Lot 15-2E on the south side of Sheppard Avenue, stretching from Bayview Avenue to Leslie Street. The relatively high purchase price of £900 and the late date tell us that the Clarks were not the first owners and that the property had been at least partially cleared by the time they took possession. The early ownership of the lot unfolded as follows:

1802	Crown grant to Joseph Provost
1804	Joseph Provost to Richard Graham
1832	Richard Graham to John Harp
1832	John Harp to Joseph Stiffens
1839	Joseph Stiffens to Robert Padgett
1841	Robert Padgett to Thomas Clark[1]

Thomas built his first log house as soon as he took possession of the land. His first wife died in 1844, after bearing seven children. Later, he would marry the apparently very brave Nancy Miller whose family farmed Lot 16-2E,

directly to the north across Sheppard Avenue. Nancy would bear Thomas six more children. (Research showed that this Thomas Clark is also referred to as Thomas Clarke in several documents, although he is not to be confused with the Clarkes of Downsview.)

The family was intensely involved in the community's religious life. Their first house, despite the seven children underfoot, had been the meeting place for the Wesleyan Methodists of Oriole, the hamlet at the corner of Leslie Street and Sheppard Avenue East. In 1853, the group would organize as "Clark's Congregation." They would hold Sunday services in the little log schoolhouse that had been built near today's Leslie and Sheppard in 1826, and later in the brick schoolhouse that was built nearby on Thomas's land in 1848. They continued to hold their meetings even when threatened with house- and barn-burnings by local gangs. Apparently the plague of gangs in Toronto is nothing new. In this case, it would appear that the cowards behind these ultimately idle threats may have had a vested interest in liquor sales in the area, as the Wesleyan Methodists were known to be allied with the Temperance movements of the day.

Courtesy of Toronto Public Library, S 1-3683B.

Regular services would continue to be held at Oriole United Church for at least a year after this 1956 photograph was taken by J.V. Salmon. Behind the little church we can see the looming bulk of the massive Rex Chainbelt factory that fronted on Sheppard Avenue East. The church was demolished in 1965, and, the factory, one of Willowdale's earliest and largest industries, would follow not long after.

In 1873, Thomas sold some of his land on the southwest corner of today's Sheppard and Old Leslie Street for the construction of a proper church. This could be considered an unusual sale, since most pioneer farmers were happy to *donate* land for such a purpose, but the details of the transaction are not known. When completed, the 1,500-square-foot, yellow-brick structure would feature gothic-style windows and an overall air of simplicity that reflected the values of the Methodist congregations of the day. One of the church's preachers was the Reverend Edwin A. Pearson, father of future Canadian prime minister, Lester B. Pearson. Initially known as the Oriole Methodist Church, the name was changed to the Oriole United Church in the mid-1920s when the property was transferred to the United Church of Canada.

The church would serve the community well for many years, until a burgeoning North York began to close in. The solemn last Sunday service was held on May 12, 1957. The congregation then transferred its Sunday services to Harrison Road Public School, one block south of William Harrison's farmhouse in York Mills. Sunday-school classes would continue to be held at the old church for a while longer until all activities of the congregation were permanently moved to the new Oriole-York Mills United Church on Bayview Avenue, just north of York Mills Road, in 1961.

The little church on Sheppard Avenue would remain alone and abandoned until 1965 when it was demolished for a strip mall that would itself be demolished just twenty years later. And so it goes....

In 1874, Thomas sold half-an-acre of his farm for the construction of a new public school to replace the one that had been built in 1848. Located next to the Oriole Methodist Church, the new red-brick schoolhouse, S.S. #11, stood until 1910, when it was replaced by the red-brick Oriole Public School. The new school was a lovely little building — well-designed, functional,

Courtesy of Toronto Public Library, S 1-3684A.

Students were still heeding the call of Oriole Public School's bell when this photo was taken by J.V. Salmon in 1956.

and in perfect harmony with its surroundings. It served the community for nearly half a century until classes were terminated in 1958. The building then served as a residence and later as office space, before being demolished in 1966 to facilitate the reconstruction of the Leslie Street and Sheppard Avenue intersection into the format that exists today. The cornerstone of the school was incorporated into the new Dunlace Public School in the new Silver Hills subdivision, a half-a-mile or so southwest across Highway 401.

In 1887, the Clarks sold their Barberry Place farm to Samuel William Armstrong, who may have been related to a William Armstrong, a farmer in the area from 1806 to 1836. When that William died in 1836, his farm was purchased by the Mulhollands, who were related by marriage. After selling

Photo by Scott Kennedy

Without caring and committed homeowners to maintain and protect Willowdale's remaining farmhouses from the ravages of the modern world, a photograph like this would not be possible. Barberry Place is pictured here on a beautiful spring day in 2010.

Barberry Place, the Clarks moved to farmland they owned on Lot 16-2E, directly to the north, where they would farm for over twenty years. The farmland of Barberry Place was not developed until sometime around 1950, when a small subdivision was built around Rean Drive and Sheppard Square. The rest of the acreage had fallen to further residential and industrial development by the time 1960 rolled around.

As for things that were *not* demolished, there is Barberry Place itself, named for the red-berried barberry bushes that once grew there in profusion. Built in 1855, and built to last, the house still stands in its original location, though almost comically dwarfed and surrounded by faux New York-style high-rise condominiums and "brownstone" townhouses. The actual construction of Barberry Place is intriguing, involving details and techniques seen in few, if any, other houses in the area.

The fieldstone foundation is eighteen inches thick. The basement floor isn't dirt; it's paved in red brick. The exterior walls are three bricks thick, painted white. All lumber used in the house is white pine, cut on the property. All wall laths are hand-split pine. Basement ceilings and verandahs are fully finished with lath and plaster. All interior trim is custom-made, hand-fitted, and unique to the house. Later additions include two gables on the front of the house that detract somewhat from the house's overall simplicity and a cottage-style addition to the rear that blends in more successfully. All other traces of Thomas Clark's farm have been obliterated, some aspects several times over. Fortunately, Barberry Place still stands on its original foundation at #9 Barberry Place on the south side of Sheppard, just east of Bayview.

At this writing, a massive redevelopment on former Canadian Tire property on the south side of Sheppard Avenue has temporarily resulted in Lot 15-2E being more vacant — that is, without any buildings on it — than at any time since the mid-twentieth century. But this situation won't last for long. In addition to the existing Canadian Tire and IKEA stores, the land will soon be home to dozens of additional retail outlets and thousands of new condo dwellers.

Chapter Seven

Lot 16-2E and the Bayview Village Plaza

IMAGINE STANDING ON THE NORTHEAST CORNER OF BAYVIEW and Sheppard, just south of the subway station, and looking east. The Bayview Village Mall, apartment buildings, and condominiums fill the entire field of vision. Now look north for a quarter-of-a-mile, past the subway station, past the condo building that thinks it's a cruise ship, and past the townhouses of the Bayview Mews, all the way to the southern edge of Bayview Gardens. Now look east again — right over to Leslie Street. This expanse of two hundred acres is Lot 16-2E, a most impressive piece of land in anyone's book. Imagine how beautiful it must have been when it was all farmland, when soft wheat bent to the wind on a hot summer day, when Jersey cows sheltered under towering elms beneath the hanging-basket nests of Baltimore orioles, when there was no sound, save for the wind and the birds.

This is the challenge of the mind, really — to imagine this land when it was all farmland. It isn't easy. It's heartbreaking sometimes. Yet, often the best way to accept the future is to picture the past.

This chapter isn't named after a farm or a farmer or a family, but the actual lot number. This seemed appropriate, as

Lot 16-2E is one of the few lots in this book that was divided among a number of families, almost from the beginning. This lot was farmed by one of the most convivial groups of farmers in Willowdale. It was farmed primarily by three families from the early 1800s into the 1950s. Thomas Clark of Barberry Place, just across Sheppard Avenue to the south, farmed part of the lot, as did William Smith, who also had a farm and a home on the former St. John's Clergy Reserve, the Glebe land granted to St. John's Anglican Church in York Mills, two lots to the south. The first family of Lot 16-2E, however, was the Millers, who farmed here for over 130 years after Jacob Miller purchased the entire lot in 1807. The families were so friendly, in fact, that Thomas Clark married his neighbour, Nancy Miller, after his first wife died in 1844.

When Jacob Miller bought the complete lot, it was almost certainly virgin field and forest. Originally granted by the Crown to a Mary Garner in 1802,[1] the lot was sold to a Christian Hendricks in 1806. When Jacob Miller acquired the spectacular property, he had to build a log cabin to shelter his family, which is a pretty strong indication that the property was still in its original condition when the Millers took possession.

By 1822, ownership of the lot had changed, with Jacob's sons James and Jacob Jr. holding separate fifty-acre parcels on the west half of the lot, while a Francis Lee appeared as owner of the eastern one hundred acres. This farm was passed down through the Lee family until 1887, including to Christopher E. Lee, whose name suggests he was part horror-movie star and part Civil War general. Christopher inherited the eastern half of the lot in 1854, by which time he had also been farming the southwest corner of Lot 8-2E, down by Post Road, for eight years — clearly a man who knew his way up and down Bayview Avenue.

One year after Christopher inherited his one hundred acres, he sold the western fifty acres to Thomas Clark. The Clarks would farm this lot for even longer than they farmed their Barberry Place farm, which they sold to Samuel William Armstrong in 1887. Francis Clark inherited part of the eastern half of Lot 16-2E from his father, Thomas, in 1883, and bought the remaining fifty-three acres from the Lee family in 1887. The Clarks would farm Lot 16-2E well into the 1930s.

As the 1890s dawned, ownership of the lot would stabilize for the next twenty years or so, with the Clarks on the eastern half, the Smiths still farming the western fifty acres of the lot that William Smith had purchased in 1871, and the Millers farming the fifty acres between the two. Other families, including members of the surveyor David Gibson's family, would occupy a ten-acre corner on the southwest of the Clarks' land until the end of the 1800s, but, by 1910, it was all down to "the firm" of Smith, Miller, and Clark.

Levi Smith first appears on the fifty-acre farm he inherited from his father, William, at the corner of Bayview and Sheppard around 1910. William's son, Jacob, inherited his farm on Lots 11 and 12-2E at the corner of Bayview and York Mills, while another son, William II, inherited his father's third farm on the former St. John's Clergy Reserve on Lot 14-2E. Levi is pictured here with his trusty sheepdog and

pitchfork. It's hard to believe that this picture, with crops in the fields and towering evergreens, was taken at the corner of Bayview and Sheppard. The other picture of Levi's farm always touches the heart. This image of little Frances Morrison dressed in her Sunday best, looking shyly down at the ground while one of Levi's Jersey cows regards her with a degree of bemusement, is what photography is all about. The fact that these two seem so alive to us now, nearly hundred years after this fleeting moment was captured, seems proof positive that time can stand still.

Joseph Miller, grandson of Jacob, pictured around 1905 in front of the house that his father James had built some sixty-five years earlier, inherited his father's fifty-acre farm in the middle of Lot 16-2E in 1882. Pictured here with his wife, daughter Edith, and two of the Webster boys who were related to the Millers by marriage, Joseph willed the farm to his children just as his father had willed it to him.

Francis Clark is shown as the sole owner of the eastern one hundred acres at the corner of Leslie and Sheppard in 1910. The accompanying photo, taken sometime in the 1920s, shows Clark family members in front of Arthur Clark's house, built on Lot 16-2E, on the north side of Sheppard Avenue East.

By the end of the Second World War, the combination of improved roads and a wave of returning servicemen eager to find new jobs and start families began to change the face of North York forever, especially along main thoroughfares like Sheppard Avenue. Portions of Lot 16-2E were beginning to be severed to create smaller parcels for businesses such as the fledgling garden centre that Len Cullen,[2] co-founder of Weall and Cullen Nurseries (now a part of Sheridan Nurseries, who still occupy this site at least until re-development, scheduled for sometime in 2014), built on the five acres of Lot 16-2E he purchased in 1948 for $900 an acre. The shed

Outside: Photographer unknown, North York Historical Society, NYHS 1036.. Inside: Photographer unknown, North York Historical Society, NYHS 1032.

There was still plenty of farming to be done on the northeast corner of Bayview and Sheppard when this photo was taken in the 1920s. Levi Smith, pictured here, would pass this farm along to his son, just as his father had passed it along to him.

It would be wonderful to know what Frances Morrison and Levi Smith's cow were trying to tell each other one summer day in the 1920s.

Photo by Ted Chirnside, Toronto Public Library, TC 24.

Will today's generation look as interesting to Willowdale residents of 2114 as Joseph Miller's family appears in this photo from the first decade of the twentieth century? Shown here are (left–right): Edith Miller, ? , Harold Webster, William Webster, and Mr. and Mrs. Joseph Miller.

that served as his original office was built on former Clark farmland, between a pigpen and an abattoir. Residential development of this area was still some time in the future, however, and while maps from the mid-1950s show both sides of Sheppard Avenue between Yonge Street and Bayview as fully subdivided, Lot 16-2E, and, indeed everything north

and east of it, was still farmland. Sadly, this bucolic situation was not to last.

Twelve acres of the Miller farm were purchased in 1951 for the construction of St. Gabriel's Catholic Church. The completed church and attached fifteen-bedroom monastery were officially opened on June 7, 1953, when Sheppard Avenue

Photographer unknown, North York Historical Society, NYHS 1039.

Hard work and perseverance seem to have paid off for Willowdale carpenter Robert J. Clark, seen on the right, and his brother-in-law, Dr. Melhuish of Toronto, as they are photographed sometime in the 1920s at the Sheppard Avenue home of Robert's brother, Arthur.

was still a two-lane country road. The church served the community well for over fifty years. Not only did its walls house a place of worship, they also engaged the community in ways that churches of today could only imagine, such as the Saturday night dances at the parish hall that attracted teenagers from all across Toronto to hear performers such as The Guess Who.

Half-a-mile north of Bayview and Sheppard, construction of the Bayview Village subdivision was underway on former farmland by 1955. A couple of years later, the much smaller Bayview Gardens subdivision was built on part of Lot 17-2E, south of today's Citation Drive. Retail outlets soon followed, including the full-fledged Weall and Cullen Garden Centre that started out as that little shed, gas stations like Gerry Balabik's Shell, and the Loblaws store that was built on the northeast corner of Bayview and Sheppard, in a muddy pit that had once been part of Levi Smith's farm. In fact, when the big yellow Loblaws with the green neon sign opened in 1959, the parking lot was such a mud pit that the store had to hire local tow-truck drivers to extricate shoppers so they could go home.

It didn't take long for this farmland on Lot 16-2E to be ingested — five years tops. No effort was made to honour or preserve anything. It was strictly "out with the old and in with the new." The outdoor Bayview Village Plaza sprouted to the east of Loblaws in 1963. Low-rise apartments were built to the east of Saint Gabriel's. A strip mall or two, more gas stations, restaurants, office buildings, the Miller Paving yards near Leslie and Sheppard — all took their bites out of Lot 16-2E until nothing remained, save for the deep valley of the East Don River on the northeast corner of Leslie and Sheppard, where development was forbidden following Hurricane Hazel.

Then the *re*-development began. The plaza was re-built into an indoor mall. High-rise apartments succeeded low-rise apartments. Townhouses took the place of detached houses. And condos — the inescapable, inevitable condos — rose and covered the land. Even Saint Gabriel's was demolished for a condominium project. The garden centre is still there and the CNR trestle across the East Don Valley, but that's about it.

Should you ever pass the corner of Bayview and Sheppard, try to remember one thing. Remember the photo of little Frances Morrison and Levi Smith's cow, and don't be surprised if you catch yourself smiling.

Chapter Eight

John D. Finch's Farm

Innkeeper and farmer John Finch may not be familiar to modern-day Torontonians, but the avenue that honours him is as familiar to them as their own names. Finch Avenue traverses almost the entire city, from the Humber River in the west to the Rouge River in the east. It is one of the busiest routes in Toronto, encompassing all aspects of our city, from the gritty urban landscape of the Jane/Finch corridor to the leafy silence of the Rouge Valley National Park.

The route was named in the late 1800s, while the Finches were still living on their farm, which ran along the north side of Finch Avenue between Yonge Street and Bayview, on the southern half of Lot 21-1E. While the family worked a relatively small farm, it would be John's other occupation that would prove the source of his immortality, for John operated two of the finest inns in the area. Quenching thirsts, filling bellies, and offering warm beds to weary travellers for nearly forty years made him one of North York's more valuable citizens, and earned him the recognition he is still afforded today.

The lot John Finch settled on had first been granted to Thomas Johnson in 1800. The Johnsons were one of the first families to settle in North York, arriving from their native Pennsylvania in the late 1700s. Thomas farmed there for eleven years, after which time the lot went through a series of uncommitted owners before John Montgomery and his father Alexander took it over in 1815. Their bizarre story is revealed in the chapter on the Montgomery/Elliot Farm.

Sometime around 1833, John Finch rented The Bird in Hand Inn from John Montgomery, who had built it in 1820 with his father's assistance, just south of today's Newtonbrook Plaza. Some six years earlier, in 1827, following a bitter family dispute and a court order, the building had been literally cut in half, with Alexander retiring to his residence in the north half of the building and John continuing to operate the tavern in the southern half. When John Finch rented the property, John Montgomery headed south to Yonge and Eglinton to build the most notorious tavern in Canada's history. By the time the Upper Canada Rebellion was launched from Montgomery's Tavern in 1837, John Finch was maintaining his neutrality and concentrating on the continuing success of The Bird in Hand. By all accounts, he did a commendable job, since his inn was held in high regard by local travellers for the excellent food, lodging, and libations it provided.

Courtesy of Toronto Public Library, TC 63.

The Bedford Park Hotel, formerly Finch's Hotel, looms over its newer neighbours on the southwest corner of Yonge Street and Fairlawn Avenue in this 1955 photograph taken by Ted Chirnside.

Photo by Barbara Sabo, North York Historical Society, NYHS 1537.

The Finch family farmhouse at 5611 Yonge Street, pictured here in early 1973, was demolished in 1977 to make way for low-rise retail and offices.

In 1847, John bought the inn and the southern half of the farm from the Montgomerys. He then closed the inn and built a new hotel on the northeast corner of Yonge and Finch. He called his new establishment Finch's Hotel and placed an advertisement in *The British Colonist* of September 20, 1848. The ad stated that John had:

> … opened a new and capacious hotel on Yonge Street, situated within a quarter of a mile of the premises formerly occupied by the subscriber.… The house and outbuildings

are entirely new.… The subscriber will always take care to have his larder well stored and his Wine and Spirit Cellar well supplied with genuine articles … his stabling shall be well regulated, so that every comfort … may at all times be depended upon at Finch's Hotel.

The new, two-storey frame hotel proved even more popular than its predecessor, becoming a destination in its own right, rather than just a stop along the way.

John continued as the proprietor of Finch's Hotel until he retired in 1860. The hotel was then leased to a series of innkeepers: Thomas Palmer in 1860, John Likens in 1864, James Fenley in 1869, and William Kirk in 1871. In 1873, John sold the hotel to Charles McBride, who dismantled it and used the timbers to build the Bedford Park Hotel on his farm at the corner of Yonge Street and Fairlawn Avenue. The hotel stood, obscured by various storefronts, until the 1980s. John Finch died in 1884, leaving the farm to his family, who continued to work the land well into the twentieth century.

The 1920s brought rapid change to North York. The advent of the automobile, more roads, and improved public transportation all conspired to make it easy for people to live in North York and work in Toronto. The rural society was being swallowed up by the urban society and nowhere was it more noticeable than along main roads such as Finch Avenue. Farmers sold individual lots for new houses and even began to subdivide their land for the construction of *blocks* of new houses. And so, piece by piece, John Finch's farm began to disappear.

Today, there is nothing left of his former farm. The Finch family farmhouses stood on the northeast corner of Yonge and Finch until they were demolished in 1977, over 140 years after John Finch signed the lease on The Bird in Hand.

Courtesy of Toronto Public Library, TC 201.

This view, captured by photographer Ted Chirnside in 1957, looking northeast across the intersection of Yonge Street and Finch Avenue, would remain surprisingly unchanged for the next twenty years. Two Finch family farmhouses stand to the north of the Bank of Nova Scotia at 5611 and 5617 Yonge Street.

Chapter Nine

The Montgomery/Elliot Farm

Some may remember the Algonquin Tavern on the east side of Yonge Street between Cummer and Finch, and likewise the Willowdale Golf Club, the Simpson Auction Barn, the Newtonbrook Airfield, and the Limberlost Riding Academy. Many are probably familiar with St. John's Rehab Hospital on Cummer Avenue or the Finch subway station with the hydro towers marching through its parking lot.

The one thing that all of these places have in common is that they were all built on the farm that John Elliot bought in 1910. More intriguing still is the realization that the farm was already over one hundred years old when John acquired it.

The history of this farm reaches all the way back to the late 1700s, when the Johnson family left their native Pennsylvania and settled in North York. Lawrence Johnson and his sons Nicholas, Thomas, Abraham, and Joseph settled on five different lots on both sides of Yonge Street, just north of the Cummer family holdings. By 1798 the family had built four log cabins and cleared ten to twelve acres of each lot in accordance with the conditions of their Crown land grants. Thomas, who settled on the southernmost Lot 21-1E was the only one who hadn't built a cabin by 1798, but he must have pulled his socks up as he was granted full deed to his land by the Crown in 1800.

Thomas would remain there until 1811, at which point an Alexander Gray's name would appear on the deed. This is a different Alexander Gray than the one who emigrated from Paisley, Scotland, in 1820 to run a number of mills near present-day Don Mills and York Mills Roads. The farm would then tumble through the hands of four different owners in four years before Alexander Montgomery and his son John bought the property in 1815. This Alexander had previously owned farms on Lot 10-2E and Lot 12-3E, near the current Leslie and York Mills. This, his third farm, would remain in the family for over thirty years, through some of the most riveting events in the history of Upper Canada.

John and his father built the first of several inns, which John would own in his lifetime, on this farm in 1820. The Bird in Hand Inn, mentioned in the previous chapter, was a two-storey frame structure built around a centre hall plan. It was an immediate success with the travellers of the day, who depended on hospitable inns every few miles to mitigate the misery of the muddy, rutted roads. Things went well for several years, before a disagreement between father and son would lead to one of the more bizarre incidents in the history of North York.

It seems that John and Alexander had been having ever more frequent arguments over the operation of the inn. In January 1827, following legal proceedings, a court order led to the inn being cut in half — literally. The structure was sawn in half, from the peak of the roof down to the ground. John continued to operate the inn in the southern portion of the building while Alexander retired to the northern part, which was now his private home. Apparently this arrangement worked well, as The Bird in Hand continued under John's ownership until the 1830s, at which time he leased the inn to John Finch and moved south to Yonge and Eglinton, where he would build the most notorious tavern in Canadian history.

Montgomery's Tavern was a two-storey frame structure on the west side of Yonge Street, just up the hill from Eglinton Avenue on one of the highest points of land in the entire area. The tavern wouldn't last long, for in 1837 the most famous battle of the Upper Canada Rebellion was fought here, and before the day was out Montgomery's Tavern would be burned to the ground.

On December 3, 1837, several hundred rebel reformers gathered at Montgomery's Tavern, most having travelled from many miles away in the cold and snow. They were mostly disenchanted farmers, fed up with the way their concerns were routinely ignored by the ruling Family Compact. Although December 7 had been chosen as the day to engage the government troops, this particular group had grown impatient. By December 5, they had run out of food and decided to march down Yonge Street themselves, without waiting for either their fellow rebels or the assigned day. On this night they were cold, tired, and armed mostly with simple farm implements. They marched down Yonge Street to Maitland Avenue, where they were met by Sheriff William Jarvis and a smaller, though much better armed government force that included twenty-seven sharpshooters.

The skirmish was brief. The rebels, severely outgunned, retreated. Both sides re-grouped, and two days later the government troops marched up Yonge Street with two cannons and numerous sharpshooters, engaging the rebels at Montgomery's Tavern. Once again, the skirmish was brief, and after a cannon ball was shot through the tavern, the rebels retreated and the loyalist commander, Lieutenant-Governor Sir Francis Bond Head, ordered the tavern burned to the ground. The tavern, intriguingly, had been rented to a John Linfoot just the week before.

When his tavern was burned to the ground, John Montgomery's family was relatively safe in Newtonbrook, about seven miles away. Nonetheless, John was arrested for his part in the uprising, as were many others. But the Rebellion worked in strange ways. Although a total failure as an actual rebellion, it would quickly lead to the government reforms that the farmers had been seeking all along. Lieutenant-Governor Sir Francis Bond Head, the de facto head of the Family Compact, was recalled to England and never held public office again. Four years after the Rebellion, the government's Durham Report would initiate many of the reforms that the farmers had fought for, and would also lay the groundwork for our current system of provincial government.

Although two of the rebels were executed for their role in the Rebellion, John Montgomery and many others were eventually pardoned by the Crown. The news reached John in the United States, where he had fled after being sentenced to banishment in Van Dieman's Land (Tasmania). John, like Thomas and Michael Shepard, had escaped from prison in Kingston while awaiting banishment, and made his way across the lake to the United States. After he was pardoned, he returned to Yonge and Eglinton, where he built a new hotel just south of the old one. He would go on to open two more hotels in downtown Toronto, while turning the Yonge and Eglinton property over to his son, William. Today's extension of Broadway Avenue west of Yonge Street is called Montgomery Avenue.

Courtesy of the Toronto Public Library, TC 68.

This moment, captured on a summer evening in the mid-1950s, by photographer Ted Chirnside, will surely bring a smile to the many North York residents who passed through this iconic front door in search of adult beverages: ladies and escorts to the main room and dance floor on the right, men only to the beverage room behind the sombre brick wall on the left. Though long considered one of the rougher taverns in the area, it wasn't such a bad place once they got to know you. The former Elliot family barn, shown to the left, disappeared nearly thirty years before last call at the Algonquin in 1986.

Meanwhile, back up in Newtonbrook, John Finch closed The Bird in Hand in 1847 and built a new hotel on the same farm, on the northeast corner of today's Yonge and Finch. Finch's Hotel operated until 1873, when it was sold to Charles McBride. He dismantled it and used the timbers to build a new hotel, the Bedford Park Hotel, on his farm, which lay south of Fairlawn Avenue on the west side of Yonge Street.

Maps of Newtonbrook show John Finch and his descendants retaining ownership of the south half of the Newtonbrook farm into the 1900s. Their one-hundred-acre parcel stretched along the north side of Finch Avenue from Yonge Street to Bayview, and, yes, they were the Finches who gave their name to the concession that formed the southern boundary of their farm. The north half of the farm would again tumble through a series of owners after the Montgomerys left, with everyone from the Bank of Canada to the Cummer family being listed as owners of one parcel or another.

The situation solidified somewhat around 1861 with John and Mary Francis owning the north half of Lot 21-1E as well as the southern half of the neighbouring lot to the north, Lot 22-1E, which reached up to Cummer Avenue. The Francises also farmed the west half of Lot 20-2E on the southeast corner of Bayview and Finch, and the magnificent Lot 32-1E in Thornhill, where the former Francis farmhouse is now known as the Heinztman House, named after a subsequent owner.[1]

When John Francis died in 1910, his sons John and Edward sold the Yonge Street farmland to John Elliot. Maps of the day show the Finch family still farming the south half of Lot 21-1E, while John Elliot is in possession of the north half of this lot, as well as the adjoining Lot 22-1E to the north, which extended up to Cummer Avenue. The east half of both lots, however, had been severed by this point, perhaps owing to the valley created by Newtonbrook Creek. Robert Risebrough owned forty-six acres of Lot 22-1E on the

southwest corner of Bayview and Cummer and a William Ford, whose descendants would farm here until the 1950s, owned an eighty-acre farm directly to the south that fronted on Bayview Avenue, where the Bayview Arena stands today. The Ford farm straddled Lots 21-1E and 22-1E.

John Elliot had emigrated from Ireland in 1860, and, in an almost exact reversal of John Montgomery's life, spent twenty years running hotels in downtown Toronto before moving north to farm in Newtonbrook. In 1910, he sold his hotels and bought the Francis farm with the intention of raising Shorthorn cattle. He hired his neighbour William MacKenzie (not the rebel leader) to build the barn shown in the photograph that would stand on Yonge Street until it was dismantled in 1958.

The farm got off to a good start, but John Ellitt suffered a stroke in 1912 and died three years later. His sons, George, Matthew, and Edward took over. Though the brothers would continue to farm, they would also become increasingly adept at finding new ways to build on their inheritance. In 1928, they opened an airfield behind the barn on Yonge Street. They also moved another barn next door to the Yonge Street barn and converted it into a home where George and Matthew lived. In 1936, they turned this structure into the Algonquin Tavern, which they operated for sixteen years before selling it in 1952.

George Elliot was also active in local politics. He was elected deputy-reeve of North York from 1929–30 and as reeve from 1931–33. He struggled through the early years of the Depression, trying to help the needy, though his hands were largely tied by the extensive international scope of the circumstances.

George had previously served in the First World War. Several years after his return he bought two of the downtown hotels that had once belonged to his father and continued to operate them until the 1940s. He was also a well-known horse breeder and rider who won many trophies in addition to judging horse shows in Canada and the United States between 1922 and 1962, the year he established a two-hundred-acre farm in Markham.

In 1929, the brothers opened the Willowdale Golf Course, which extended east from Yonge Street to the Newtonbrook Creek ravine. An old farmhouse was turned into a luxurious clubhouse with the addition of two new wings. The clubhouse featured separate mens' and ladies' lounges, as well as a grand dining room and elaborate landscaping. Still, the brothers weren't satisfied, so they hired Stanley Thompson, Canada's pre-eminent golf-course architect, to turn their course into something special. When it opened in 1931 as the rechristened Willowdale Golf Club, the 165-acre layout was recognized as the first course in the province to conform to the regulations of the newly-formed Ontario Golf Association. George and Matthew would continue to operate the Willowdale Golf Club for the next twenty-five years. George died at his farm in Markham in 1971.

Meanwhile, the brothers continued to find new ways to improve the cash crop from their father's farm. In 1932, they sold thirty-two acres to Ontario Hydro for the power lines, which can still be seen marching across the property today. In 1934, they sold twenty-five acres on the north side of the farm to the Sisters of St. John for a convalescent hospital that opened in 1937 and continues to serve the community as a state-of-the-art rehabilitation facility to this day.

The hospital can trace its roots all the way back to 1884 and the founding of the Anglican Sisterhood of St. John the Divine — the first all-Canadian order in the country. The very next year, the sisters opened a hospital in Moose Jaw, Saskatchewan, to tend to the victims of the bloody Riel Rebellion. After the rebellion was put down later that year, they returned to Toronto and opened a women's hospital on Major Street, near College and Spadina. This hospital operated until the 1930s, when the sisters were convinced by Vincent Massey, soon to be Canada's first native-born governor-general, and the highly regarded hospital consultant, Dr. Harvey Agnew, to open a convalescent hospital. They were assisted in their efforts by numerous fundraising events and a generous legacy.

The sisterhood vacated their downtown hospital, which would then operate as Doctors' Hospital until the end of the century, and moved to the new St. John's Convalescent Hospital on the twenty-five acres on Cummer Avenue that they had purchased from the Elliots for $18,000. There was still work to be done however, and more years and fundraisers would pass before the new hospital was fully furnished and equipped. It stands there to this day, still serving the community with a slightly updated name.

The Elliots were good neighbours and would often take their horses and sleighs over to the hospital to take the patients of St. John's out for sleigh rides in the wintertime. The remaining Elliot land was leased to the Limberlost Riding Academy and later to the operators of the Simpson Auction Barn.

The Willowdale Golf Club was sold to developers in 1958 to become the Newtonbrook subdivision. The Algonquin Tavern would continue to quench thirsts until it too was demolished in 1986, taking with it the last trace of John Elliot's farm. People can still walk the open portion of the hydro right-of-way, however, from Willowdale Avenue all the way over to Bayview, and, in so doing, gain a new appreciation for the farmers who once worked this beautiful land.

CHAPTER TEN

Mazo de la Roche, Brébeuf, and the Zoroastrians

RESEARCH INTO THE HISTORY OF THIS FARM REVEALED AN amazing depth of layer upon layer of history. From Crown lands granted before the War of 1812 to Mayor Mel Lastman in the swingin' seventies, the stories unravelled with such unpretentious ease that it was almost like watching a television program. This lot, Lot 25-1E, must have been breathtaking when it was granted to Richard Lawrence in 1808. It's a long way from the southeast corner of Yonge and Steeles, east to Willowdale Avenue and all the way down the big hill to the valley of the East Don River at Bayview Avenue. Still an impressive sight today, this piece of land would have been even more impressive when Richard first gazed upon it in its original state.

Land records indicate just what a daunting task it was to clear and farm this land, as they tell us that seven years after being granted the property, Richard sold the east half to Alexander Gray, who had previously owned part of the Montgomery/Elliot farm four lots to the south. In 1819, Richard sold the west half of Lot 25-1E to a John D. Baldwin. The lot would never be reunited under one owner again, although a couple of families would demonstrate their loyalty to the place by farming their separate halves for generations.

James Robinson set the longest stretch of family involvement when he bought Alexander Gray's farm in 1823. The Robinsons were still farming there over 130 years later. George Crookshank, whose story is told more completely in the chapter on Lot 24-1E, bought John Baldwin's farm on the west half of the lot in 1837. Although records indicate that this farm was owned by Julia Lambert in 1860, after George Crookshank's death (and sold to Stephen Heward in 1868 and farmed by Stephen's son in 1892), maps from 1910 show the farm in possession of the "Cruikshank" Estate. (George Crookshank married Sarah Lambert in 1821. Their only daughter, Catherine, married into the Heward family).

Other records from Thornhill and North York confirm the name change from Crookshank to Cruikshank. The same 1910 maps show a P.W. Burton farming on the east half of Lot 25-1E on the Bayview-end of the property.

In the early 1930s, a portion of the Burton farm on the southwest corner of Bayview and Steeles was sold to a Mrs. Lands from Hamilton who, in 1933, built a house there, which she used as a summer retreat. Consider that for a minute — a woman from Hamilton coming to North York for her summer vacation! That says something about just how bucolic North York really was, not all that long ago. Mrs. Land's country idyll didn't last long, however, and, in 1939, she sold the property to Mazo de la Roche, one of the most successful authors in Canadian history, and also a woman of considerable mystery. Even her name was a fabrication.

Mazo Roche was born in Newmarket on January 15, 1879. Her father owned a general store in town, but, despite his best efforts, the store failed when little Mazo was only six. The family then moved to Toronto where Mr. Roche never seemed to find any employment that lasted for more than a year or two. In 1910, the family moved to Bronte, near Oakville, where Mazo, now a spinster past her thirtieth birthday, would find the inspiration she needed to forge a new life for herself. She had already realized some moderate success as a writer of short stories and now, inspired by a nearby house called Benares, she began to formulate her image of a fictitious family she called the Whiteoaks of Jalna.

When Mazo Roche began to seriously consider a career as a writer, she changed her name to Mazo de la Roche. She now claimed to be descended from French aristocracy, with a mysterious drop of Irish blood. By 1927, she had written several reasonably successful novels and moved to a flat at 86 Yorkville Avenue in Toronto, which she shared with her cousin Caroline Clement.

Caroline had been taken in by Mazo's family when she was just a child and almost immediately became Mazo's lifelong companion. After the couple moved to Toronto, Caroline took a government job to provide them with some financial stability and also accepted additional duties as Mazo's accountant, typist, manager, and editor. That same year, all hell broke loose as the literary world beat a path to the door of that second-floor flat in Yorkville when *Atlantic Monthly* announced that they had awarded Mazo de la Roche their annual prize for novel of the year. The prize was

$10,000 — in 1927 dollars.—when such a sum would have been enough to buy three detached, brick houses in central Toronto. The novel was *Jalna*.

Mazo was now forty-eight years old. Hers had not been an overnight success, but suddenly she was an international phenomenon. Reporters from all over North America journeyed to Toronto in hopes of being granted an interview. The City of Toronto honoured her with a banquet. All in all, it was too much for such a reclusive person. Shortly after the initial hoopla died down, Caroline quit her job and the two women left for an extended European vacation — so extended in fact that they did not return to Canada for several years.

After travelling through continental Europe, the couple settled near London, in the vicinity of Windsor Castle, in a Tudor mansion called Vale House. Once they were settled in, Mazo set to work adapting her novel for the London stage. Renamed "Whiteoaks," the production ran for a record-breaking three years before touring Canada and the United States with Ethel Barrymore in one of the starring roles. In 1931, the novel was turned into a feature film that still pops up on evening television.

While in England, Mazo and Caroline decided that they would like to adopt two children, but their request was met with formidable resistance because, in the parlance of the times, two spinsters just didn't go about adopting children. It was only through the intervention of Mazo's publisher (and future British prime minister) Harold Macmillan that the women were able to realize their dreams by adopting a daughter named Esmée and a son, René. The two women adored the English country lifestyle, but the war clouds that loomed in 1939 forced them to head for home.

Upon their return to Canada, they set out to duplicate the country life they had enjoyed so much in England. They chose North York as the place to do so when they purchased Mrs. Land's summer house at Bayview and Steeles. The house as constructed

Courtesy of North York Historical Society, NYHS 1417.

Surely one of the most beautiful homes ever constructed in the current city of Toronto and still standing on its original height of land at Bayview and Steeles, "Windrush Hill" is pictured here in this 1961 photo by Lorna Gardner.

in 1933 was a little too square and stodgy for the couple's taste, so they added new wings to the east and west sides of the house, embellished with impressive Tudor details. The west wing housed garages and servants' quarters while the east wing was dominated by a spectacular English-style library with an eighteen-foot ceiling and a soaring, floor-to-ceiling bay window. The library's interior was panelled in hand-carved dark oak and featured two fireplaces with carved mantelpieces, one on the east wall and one on the north wall, where Mazo did much of her writing. A hidden door next to this fireplace led to the master bedroom on the second floor. A balcony off the master bedroom looked down into the library below. Mazo named the new estate "Windrush Hill."

Life at Windrush Hill was all that Caroline and Mazo had hoped it would be. The children swam in the East Don in summertime and skated on it in the winter. The family added some dogs to the mix and the forested grounds became the scene of many childhood adventures. They welcomed other artists into their home including Angus Macdonald, who lived in the former Benjamin Fish gristmill on the northeast corner of Bayview and Steeles, where the gas station stands today, and whose stained glass would grace such edifices as the original Sunnybrook Hospital. The family maintained the country lifestyle by doing their shopping in Thornhill rather than Toronto. In the summer they enjoyed riding their bikes on the generally empty two-lane dirt roads that were Bayview and Steeles back then. Mazo continued her prolific series of Jalna novels, but country life was not without its drawbacks.

The isolation meant that winters could be cold and lonely, never more so than when the family was snowed in. During those times, there was often no way to reach the outside world other than to strap on snowshoes and walk to Yonge Street to catch a radial car. Remember that there were few snowploughs and no buses serving the area around Bayview and Steeles until the 1950s. In addition, the huge house was extremely difficult to heat, and the outdoor oil tank and over-worked furnace failed numerous times. Mazo de la Roche was also beginning to be plagued by the health problems that would follow her for the rest of life, most notably a chronic kidney infection and arthritis. There were also problems getting domestic staff to agree to such isolation, and, when the children grew to school age, their transportation provided some unique problems as well. Esmée attended Havergal College at Lawrence and Avenue Road while René was enrolled at Upper Canada College, even further south. Most of the family's wartime gas ration was used up transporting the children to and from school. Gas rationing also made local delivery compa-

nies reluctant to travel so far out of town. The first problem was solved when Esmée and René took up residence at their respective schools, but this soon presented a new problem.

As the children grew older they began to resent the isolation of Windrush Hill and crave the excitement of the city that their school friends enjoyed as a matter of course. By 1945 all of these various problems made it clear to Mazo that she would have to abandon her dream of a country estate and move into the city. It could have been worse. The family's financial stability meant that they had their pick of virtually any house in Toronto. They first moved to a house on Russell Hill Road before finally settling into another Tudor-style house that still stands at 3 Ava Crescent in Forest Hill — the same crescent where Group of Seven artist Lawren Harris lived until he left Ontario in 1934. (His awe-inspiring art deco mansion still stands at 2 Ava Crescent.) Caroline and Mazo's days at Windrush Hill had been eerily book-ended by the Second World War.

Mazo de la Roche's last days were dominated by her health problems, although she never let her fans see her suffer. She died in 1961 after spending the last months of her life in a wheelchair. She died working on the seventeenth Jalna novel. In her lifetime she sold an astonishing ten million books. She was once the most widely read author in all of France and was so revered in Norway that people named their children and pets after characters in her novels. Her books were bestsellers in the United States and have never gone out of print in Great Britain, where even members of the Royal Family have proven to be devoted fans. Queen Mary once requested a signed copy of *The Master of Jalna*; a request that Mazo was only too happy to honour with a one-off, hand-tooled leather volume that she designed and paid for herself. Years later, King George VI declined the offer of a Jalna novel, saying that both he and the Queen had already read it. Their daughter, Queen Elizabeth II, was also a fan of these remarkable books that piqued her early interest in the dominion she would one day rule. Mazo often said that the only country in the world that never appreciated her was Canada — to which thousands of other Canadian artists would add a resounding "Amen." Interestingly, her books are currently being kept in print in Canada and have become very popular as e-books.[1] The spirit of Mazo de la Roche is now very much alive for a whole new generation of readers.

Shortly before she died, Mazo de la Roche wrote an account of her life that curiously ended with her arrival at Windrush Hill. Perhaps this was her way of refusing to accept the fact that she had been unable to import and maintain the English country lifestyle she had tried so hard to reconstruct in her native country. One of her biographers, Ronald Hambleton, who was often thwarted by her family in his effort to tell her story, once said that "her chief significance is as 'the last mourner for the dying English influence in Canada.'"[2]

Mazo de la Roche was laid to rest in 1961 in the breathtakingly beautiful cemetery of St. George's Anglican Church on Hedge Road, just east of Jackson's Point, high on a cliff overlooking the blue waters of Lake Simcoe. A stained glass window in the church, depicting St. Francis of Assisi and the animals that Mazo loved so much is dedicated to her memory. One of her neighbours there is Stephen Leacock, the only Canadian author of the time who had more readers than she did. Her papers and diaries were burned, as per her request. Caroline Clement lived in the house on Ava Crescent until she died in 1972 and was laid to rest beside Mazo. By this time, Windrush Hill was surrounded by subdivisions. It was still as beautiful as ever though, on its wooded hilltop, and still a private home. The family that bought the property from Mazo and Caroline added a sunroom, pool, and landscaped gardens.

Meanwhile, back on the portion of Lot 25-1E on Yonge Street, the farmland had been subdivided and developed shortly after the end of the Second World War. Like almost every lot in this area, it was subdivided sequentially as development flowed east and west from Yonge Street, since this was the only street that had public transit running into the city. By 1947, aerial photos show the northwest corner of Lot 25-1E covered in detached houses from Yonge Street to Willowdale Avenue and south to Newton Drive. Development would continue in an easterly direction throughout the 1950s and '60s.

In 1963, Brébeuf College School was constructed, just west of Conacher Drive, under the direction of Jesuit priests, to provide a high-school education for Catholic boys in the community. The school was named after Roman Catholic missionary Father Jean de Brébeuf, who had settled in Huronia, near Penetanguishene, on the shores of Georgian Bay in 1634. He is remembered today as the composer of the popular "Huron Carol," and as a martyr. The tragic story of his being captured and tortured to death by the Iroquois during their attack on the Hurons in 1649 is too brutal to be conveyed here. The St. Agnes Catholic Elementary School opened just to the south of Brébeuf College, and the Lillian Street Public School was built four streets to the west. Since no one opens schools without potential pupils, the transformation of the surrounding farmland to detached housing was occurring simultaneously.

By the mid-1970s, Windrush Hill had fallen into unsympathetic hands. JFM Developments Limited had purchased the house and its surrounding nine-plus acres for $1,600,000, and submitted a plan to the North York Planning Board that called for the demolition of the house to make way for a new subdivision. The planning board approved the plan but North York Council granted a six-week reprieve to see if the house could be saved while the acreage around it was developed. Local resident Marilyn Herz tried to raise money to buy the house and convert it to a museum but did not have enough time to reach her goal.

After North York Alderman Mike Smith persuaded council to talk to the developers about saving the house, Mayor Mel

Photo by Ted Chirnside, Toronto Public Library, TC 54-C.

If ever a photo could show just how much things can change in one person's lifetime, this one, taken in 1956 from the former Mazo de la Roche property, could well be it. The East Don River is shown passing beneath the concrete bow-string bridge that carried the two dirt lanes of Bayview Avenue to the jog at Steeles Avenue East, where the white car is heading west. The Benjamin Fish gristmill, in the centre, was constructed in 1832 and demolished in 1965. It was partnered with the miller's house to the right, where farmers, who travelled long distances to have their grain ground, would often spend the night.

Lastman, who initially had washed his hands of the problem, despite a flood of letters to save the house, somehow managed to broker a deal that saw millionaire Don Mills developer Harry Winton purchasing the house and an additional 1.3 acres of land from JFM for $320,000. This was in late May of 1976. There were smiles all around as Harry declared his intention of turning the two-acre property into a mini-Edwards Gardens, with the library converted to a Mazo de la Roche museum, while the Winton family lived in the rest of the house. The mayor claimed that the house would become a showpiece for North York.

Harry Winton soon got down to the business of renovating his new home while New Style Construction, JFM's partners in the eight-acre subdivision, prepared to build their subdivision. By June of 1977, Harry's renovations were complete, while the subdivision was still under construction. Up until now things had proceeded in a civilized fashion, but, by mid-June, Harry and New Style were at each others' throats. Harry, himself a developer, had allowed New Style an access road through his property to facilitate the construction of the subdivision, but when New Style cut down a row of forty-foot-tall pine trees near the border of the two properties, Harry closed the access road. The row of trees, known as the Whispering Pines, had afforded Windrush Hill a degree of isolation from the new subdivision and after they were cut down, Harry was so infuriated that he put the house up for sale.

Windrush Hill was advertised for sale in the *Globe and Mail* on August 12, 1977 for $600,000 as a war of words erupted between Harry and the Borough of North York that would last for over six months. Harry claimed he was turned down by the borough when he tried to re-zone the house as a museum — bizarrely, as an Estonian Art Centre Museum, not a Mazo de la Roche museum. Mel Lastman said Harry never applied for re-zoning. Harry then said he never applied because the process would have taken a year. Harry blamed a lack of borough cooperation when he put the

house up for sale. Alderman Mike Smith countered that Harry had been much more difficult to deal with than the borough and suggested that Harry was crying crocodile tears since he stood to realize a $100,000 profit from the sale of the house. A group of nuns from Boston expressed interest in the house as a retreat, but the borough turned them down.

In October of 1977, Harry Winton, unable to find a buyer, applied for a demolition permit, which was granted. The same week, the permit was cancelled by building commissioner Sam Beckett and borough solicitor Charles Onley, who pointed out that Harry had signed an agreement not to demolish the house for at least twenty years. It seems that then, as now, the left and right hands of government are frequently unaware of what the other hand is up to. Harry said he'd sue, but apparently he never did.

The following February, Harry accepted an offer from the Zoroastrian Society of Ontario to purchase the property. Sam Beckett signed a letter on February 17 to confirm that a place of worship was an acceptable use of the property under the then-current bylaws. That same day, Harry accepted the offer to purchase. On February 27, North York Council passed a new bylaw to restrict the property to single-family use after receiving over 250 letters expressing concerns about increased traffic and congestion.

The bylaw was enacted with unusual rapidity — one council meeting with no prior notice — in spite of the fact that Charles Onley stated that the borough had violated the Planning Act by not informing Harry and the Zoroastrian Society of the meeting and the proposed rezoning. The Zoroastrian Society went ahead with the purchase on the basis of Sam Beckett's letter of approval and were not challenged by the borough.

Today, Windrush Hill is a Zoroastrian temple, and, since full Zoroastrian congregations only meet a few times a year, the blame for the current traffic woes that despoil the once-idyllic intersection of Bayview and Steeles must be laid at someone else's feet.

CHAPTER ELEVEN

Cameron, Munshaw, Thorne, Crookshank, and Brumwell

THIS SOUNDS LIKE A LAW FIRM, DOESN'T IT? IN REALITY, IT was a spectacular farm with a parade of equally spectacular owners. This farm extended all the way from Yonge Street to Bayview Avenue, one-quarter-of-a-mile south of Steeles. As such, it was only one lot south of North York's border with Thornhill, so it comes as no surprise to learn that most of the farmers listed above actually lived and farmed in Thornhill while farming this land as well. Benjamin Thorne, in particular, stands out since Thornhill was named after him. George Crookshank built the magnificent clay and straw-brick house now known as Heintzman House, on Bay Thorn Drive in Thornhill. German immigrant Balcer Munshaw drove his oxcart to Upper Canada from the United States in 1794, and John Brumwell was one of the five farmers who petitioned the province for the creation of North York in 1922.

In the early days of settlement in Upper Canada, one impenetrable swath of virgin forest was much the same as the next. It was difficult to tell where one jurisdiction began and another ended — only that there were a lot of trees and bugs and bears and wolves and snow. Even the lot numbers reflected the borderless state that existed until the twentieth century.

Starting with Lot #1 at Eglinton and Yonge and running all the way up to Lot #35 at Langstaff Road, the numbering system transcended the borders that are recognized today.

When the Crown granted Lot 24-1E to Hugh Cameron in 1801, Balcer Munshaw and his family were already established in Thornhill where he had been granted Lot 35-1E, running along the south side of today's Langstaff Road from Yonge Street to Bayview Avenue. Hugh Cameron would only retain ownership of his land grant for two years, but the Munshaws would prevail for a lot longer than that. Mrs. Munshaw served the pioneer community as a midwife, at a time when it was necessary to ride all the way down to the town of York to summon a doctor when needed. It's a good thing she had learned this trade, as her own daughter Susan is thought to be the first white child born in the wilderness now known as Markham.

Balcer Munshaw was elected constable for Vaughan and Markham in 1799. In 1809, he built a new frame house for his growing family and donated his old log cabin for the first school in the area. The schoolteacher was John Langstaff, who had recently arrived on horseback from 550 miles away in New Jersey. He had only come for a visit but decided to stay. Two hundred years later, Langstaff Road remains to remind us of him.

The Munshaws' sons, George and Jacob, wasted little time expanding the family's holdings in a southerly direction. Jacob bought Lot 27-1W, two lots north of Steeles, running from Yonge Street to Bathurst Street along the route that the CN rail line follows today. His farm became a favourite camping spot for Native people from the north as they journeyed up and down the primitive track that was Yonge Street. This interaction did much to cement positive relations between the two groups. Jacob would remain on this farm beyond the 1867 Confederation.

In 1811, the Munshaw brothers took a bite out of North York when Jacob bought the east half of Lot 24-1E and George bought the west half. Here again, Jacob would prove the more diligent of the two, farming his half until 1865 when he handed it over to his son Nicholas, who farmed there until the early 1890s before selling the land to John Brumwell. George only held on to the western half of the lot until 1815, a scant four years. Benjamin Thorne bought George's former farmland in 1833. (In the interval between 1815 and 1833, the west half of the lot was owned by an Orm Hale and then a John Endicott.) Although most of Thorne's tale unfolds in the town that would come to bear his name, it can now also be told here since he owned one of the farms of Willowdale.

Benjamin Thorne was twenty-six years old when he followed his brother-in-law from Dorset, England, to Upper Canada in 1820. He was born the same year that Balcer Munshaw drove his oxcart to Upper Canada. Benjamin settled on Lot 32-1W, where the Thornhill Golf and Country Club stands today. Described as a man "of capital and enterprise,"[1] he built a five-storey gristmill, considered the largest in Canada at the time, as well as a tannery, a general store, and a fine brick house near the top of the hill. By 1830, he had already started a successful import-export business in the town of York, exporting flour to Great Britain and importing iron ore and household goods into Upper Canada. By all accounts, Benjamin was a kind-hearted entrepreneur, always willing to extend credit to the struggling settlers who frequented his store in York. He was also the first man in Upper Canada to pay cash for wheat, further endearing himself to the pioneer farmers.

In 1829, Benjamin petitioned for a post office in the community that would soon bear his name. At the time, residents of the little community had to travel all the way to York to pick up their mail, a round-trip journey that could take up to eight hours. His request was granted and the new post office was the first institution to bear the name "Thornhill." William Parsons, the brother-in-law that Benjamin had followed to Upper Canada a decade earlier, was appointed postmaster, a position he would hold until one year before his death in 1861.

In 1830, Benjamin married Anna Maria Willcocks, the woman who had inspired him to build that fine brick house. It was also in 1830 that Benjamin donated land on his farm for the construction of the Holy Trinity Anglican Church, an affiliation that Benjamin shared with members of Upper Canada's ruling Family Compact. Most of the farmers at that time were Methodists.

By 1836, Thornhill was a thriving community of three hundred souls with four churches to save them, whatever their affiliation. Benjamin's flour mill was so busy that, despite its size, farmers were often lined up until ten o'clock at night, waiting to have their wheat ground. Business, quite literally, could not have been better and would continue in such a fashion for the next decade. In 1842, the first year that banks could freely establish branches in both halves of the newly united Province of Canada, Benjamin was appointed one of two presidents (one for Upper Canada and one for Lower Canada) of the Bank of Montreal, which had been founded in 1817. He laid the cornerstone for the bank's building at the corner of

Photo by Scott Kennedy

The house that Balcer Munshaw built to replace his log cabin in 1809, as it looked on September 16, 2011. He seems to have done a pretty good job.

Yonge Street and Front Street in 1845, which was replaced in 1885 by the wonderfully ornate bank building that currently houses the Hockey Hall of Fame at the same location. Two years earlier, Benjamin and partner John Barwick had bought the already established Red Mill at Holland Landing to take some of the pressure off the mill at Thornhill. Three years later, things would go horribly wrong.

In 1846, following the Irish Potato Famine, Britain repealled her so-called "Corn Laws," which had allowed Canadian wheat and flour to enter Great Britain duty-free. The British, desperate for *any* food to feed their starving citizens, now dropped their tariffs on grain imports altogether. The advantage that Canadian producers had long enjoyed evaporated overnight. As countries closer to Great Britain began to take advantage of this unexpected windfall, Benjamin Thorne was literally left with shiploads of unsaleable flour. While other smaller millers were better able to absorb the blow, Benjamin's operations were so massive that the loss of his sole customer spelled certain doom. He put his mills up for sale, but there were no takers. Trustees, acting on behalf of his creditors, seized his assets in 1848. His sudden ruin very nearly destroyed the entire village, since farmers from miles around no longer had anyone to buy their wheat.

On June 2, 1848, an auction was held to dispose of some of Benjamin's more liquid assets such as wagons, sleighs, carts, hogs, and horses. The auction of the mills, house, and stores was soon to follow. The month after the first dispersal, a beaten Benjamin Thorne walked into the pasture behind his house and shot himself. He was fifty-four years old with a wife and eight children.

George Crookshank was born in New York City in 1773, where his United Empire Loyalist father, the owner and captain of a merchant sailing ship, found himself *persona-non-grata* after the British were defeated in the Revolutionary War. The family fled to New Brunswick, where George found his first employment on the family's ships sailing to the West Indies. In 1796, George and his sister Rachel followed their married sister to Upper Canada. Here, the Crookshanks finally found a welcoming home where George was granted 1,200 acres of land spread over several parcels in York Township, both inside and outside the Town of York, as soon as he arrived.

George's older sister Catherine was married to John McGill, who had been put in charge of stores and provisions for the fledgling town of York in 1792. George benefitted enormously from his connections and the good will

extended to the family by Lieutenant Governor John Graves Simcoe and his wife, Elizabeth. George was charged with provisioning Fort York and the other forts in the area. He performed his duties well and was rewarded with a series of promotions, including a promotion to receiver general in 1819 and a directorship at the Bank of Upper Canada. The bill to establish the Bank of Upper Canada had just been passed by the Legislative Assembly in 1819, although its charter was not confirmed until 1821.

George Crookshank was elected to the Legislative Council in 1821, where he would serve for twenty years. He built a town house on Peter Street and established a farm in the wilderness near Bloor and Bathurst. The road he cut through the forest in front of his farm was called Crookshank's Lane, until after George's death when it was renamed Bathurst Street in recognition of Lord Bathurst, secretary of state for war and the colonies from 1812–27. During the War of 1812, George's farmhouse was looted and commandeered by American troops, and, though he reclaimed his farm after the Americans were finally defeated, he began to shop around for a more peaceful piece of property.

In 1817, George bought Lot 32-1E in Thornhill for £750. Here he built one of the finest homes in the Greater Toronto Area. Known today as Heintzman House, named after a subsequent owner, the thirteen-room clay-and-straw-brick house is still a landmark in the community and frequently hosts a variety of functions.

This lot had originally been granted to Anthony Hollingshead in 1798. Anthony was another Loyalist who had served as an officer in the American Revolutionary War. Unlike many other Loyalist grantees, Anthony actually cleared part of his land and built a log house on the property as the Crown required, receiving his deed in 1802. His house survives to this day, although it will never be seen again. It

Photo by Scott Kennedy

Local history buffs could find few more rewarding outings than a trip to the Heinztman House, seen here in 2011. The ongoing restoration has won several awards, and though a small entrance fee is sometimes charged for the times when the house is open to the public, it is comforting to know that all funds collected go to the upkeep of the house.

seems that George Crookshank incorporated the two large rooms of the Hollingshead house into the much larger house that he built around it. When completed, the Crookshank house had no peers. For starters, the rooms were huge, with several measuring sixteen feet by twenty-five feet. A winding staircase led from the main floor to the second floor. The interior trim was custom-made from imported English walnut — at considerable expense. The massive front door was also made from English walnut and featured a twelve-inch wrought-iron lock that was opened by a seven-inch iron key. The straw-brick walls were nearly two feet thick and can be seen today through a little trap door in the parlour that affords the modern-day visitor a tell-tale glimpse of this sadly neglected method of construction, which kept the house warm in winter and cool in summer. In 1817, the same year George built his new house, he also bought a farm in North York described as Lot 25-1W, on the south side of today's Steeles, between Yonge and Bathurst.

In 1821, the Honourable George Crookshank, as he was known after his ascension to the Legislative Council, married Sarah Lambert of New York. George and Sarah, who had inherited property in the United States from her family, had three children — two sons and one daughter. In 1837, the Crookshanks bought the west half of Lot 25-1E, directly across Yonge Street from their farm on Lot 25-1W, and in 1852 they completed their North York holdings when they bought the west half of Lot 24-1E that had previously been owned, albeit briefly, by George Munshaw and Benjamin Thorne. George Crookshank was known for his kindness and his generous donations to a variety of charities. The family enjoyed a comfortable life on their Thornhill farm until George's health began to fade around 1850. He sold the family properties in town in 1851, which were subsequently subdivided and developed until all traces of the family in Toronto had disappeared.

George died in 1859. He left his entire estate to his only surviving child, daughter Catherine Crookshank Heward. Excluding the farms in Thornhill and North York, George's estate was valued at the rather staggering amount of £49,986. After Catherine sold the Thornhill farm, it passed through a number of hands before being purchased in 1881 by John Francis, who was also farming in Newtonbrook at the time.

The Francises named their new property "Sunnyside Manor Farm" and owned the farm for nearly fifty years, with Samuel Francis taking over from his father in 1882. They raised sheep and cattle and fished in the spring-fed stream that ran through the property behind their house. Their fields were full of wheat, oats, and barley and, lest it be thought that people who lived in such a grand house were somehow above their neighbours, it is known that Samuel's wife, Mary, sold her hand-churned butter for ten cents a pound and fresh eggs for ten cents a dozen. Harvest time saw an additional fourteen or fifteen hired hands sitting down at mealtime. William Francis, one of Samuel's brothers, manufactured Francis Ready-Mixed Paints at Queen and Sherbourne Streets. The company's name would eventually be changed to Benjamin Moore and Company.

In 1894, the Francises rented Sunnyside Manor Farm to another farmer and moved to a smaller farm they owned on the northeast corner of Yonge and Steeles. They returned to Thornhill in 1904 and retired to a new house they had built at the end of their lane on Yonge Street in 1916. A Mr. Royston and his son Arthur ran Sunnyside Manor Farm for the Francises until the farm was sold to Charles Theodore Heintzman in October of 1929 for $100,000. Charles was the grandson of Theodore August Heintzman, who had established the family's piano-manufacturing business in Toronto in 1860. Samuel Francis died in 1937 and his wife Mary followed him in 1944. They had been married since 1882.

Charles Heintzman was also a dedicated farmer and wasted little time putting his own stamp on the place. He made the farmhouse even more grand with the addition of a new main entrance that includes the columned porte-cochere and covered second-floor balcony that still enchant the visitor to this day. He also added garages, servants' quarters, a bar, a billiards room, and the lovely glass conservatory to the south of the house with its radiators hidden beneath the planting areas. Charles even installed an intercom system to connect the main house with the barns and other outbuildings. The farm remained a serious working farm for the next three decades, its claim to fame being the Heintzman's herd of prize-winning Jersey cattle. Charles died at home in 1954. His wife Marion followed a few years later, and, in 1959, their beautiful farm was sold to developers for $880,000.

The farm was then covered in new houses by the Costain Development Company and Wycliffe Homes. The old farmhouse stood forlorn and abandoned, while the land surrounding it was ploughed under. By the mid-1960s, the rest of Sunnyside Manor Farm had been converted to housing, and the developers turned their attention to the farmhouse and its remaining acreage where they wanted to build a high-rise apartment building. Thankfully, concerned local residents managed to convince Markham Township Council to step in and save the house as a centennial project in 1967. Markham bought the property from the developers and adapted it to fill a new role as a community centre.

The Thornhill Lions Club aided the project by working hard to find and donate suitable period furnishings to complete the project. Thanks to a dedicated team of volunteers, Heintzman House is still very much in demand for weddings, parties, meetings, fundraisers, and other events. The house was designated as a historic site under the Ontario Heritage Act in 1984 and has recently won numerous awards from the Town of Markham for the accuracy and quality of its ongoing restoration. Though not open to the public on a daily basis, Heintzman House holds many events that are open to all, such as the Christmas craft show in mid-November. The house still stands at 135 Bay Thorn Drive over two hundred years after Anthony Hollingshead started it all by proudly carving his log cabin out of the foreboding wilderness.

That leaves John Brumwell, whose exploits are also detailed in the chapter on the Risebrough family. His contribution was so seminal to North York, however, that it bears repeating. In 1894, John Brumwell, also spelled "Brummel" in some records,

bought the east half of Lot 24-1E that had been farmed by the Munshaws since 1811. While he farmed his land, he watched with dismay as fewer and fewer farmers were being elected to the council of York Township, as the population of the city of Toronto grew larger and larger. In 1919, there were no farmers elected at all, even though they were paying nearly 25 percent of the township's taxes. As noted earlier, in 1921, John and fellow disgruntled farmers, W.C. Snider, Roy Risebrough, James Muirhead, and W.J. Buchanan, climbed into Roy's Model-T Ford and criss-crossed the area, gathering signatures and support for their petition to secede from York Township and form their own township. Their efforts were successful and on the thirteenth of June, 1922, the provincial government granted their request and the Township of North York was born. John lived in a farmhouse that the Munshaws built on Bayview Avenue, across the street from today's St. Joseph's Convent and high school, which has recently been sold to another religious order, the Tyndale College and Seminary. John Brumwell's descendants farmed this land until the middle of the twentieth century, when it was sold for housing.

Benjamin Thorne's house outlived him by 115 years. After Benjamin's death, the house burned but was not destroyed. John Langstaff, who by now had abandoned his teaching career in favour of manufacturing shingles and eavestroughs, grafted the upper floor of another abandoned house onto the Thorne house to create a functional, yet extremely odd-looking new dwelling. In later years this structure housed the Thornhill Mineral Springs Resort before becoming the clubhouse of the Thornhill Golf Club, which opened on May 24, 1922, with a course designed by Canada's foremost golf course architect, Stanley Thompson. When the club became the Thornhill Golf and Country Club, the poor old house was demolished in 1963 to make room for curling rinks, lounges, locker rooms, and a new dining room.

This house was built by Jacob Munshaw on Bayview Avenue, on the eastern border of Lot 24-1E. It is pictured here around 1910 when it was owned by John Brumwell, with John's wife, Jane (Kennedy) Brumwell, standing on the back porch.

Photographer unknown, North York Historical Society, NYHS 789

Balcer Munshaw died in 1830. He and his wife were proud grandparents to forty-three grandchildren — clearly a family with few intimacy issues. Their second house, built in 1809 to replace the family's log cabin, still stands at 10 Ruggles Avenue, which runs south from Langstaff Road, just east of Yonge Street. It survived as a private residence for over 175 years, but has now been reduced to industrial office space.

It is fortunate that two of the houses built by these pioneers still exist, and although they don't exist in North York, they are close enough that they are certainly worth a visit. In addition, there is another Heinztman house still standing in North York. It was built by one of Charles's sons in the late 1940s on former Harrison family farmland and has recently been renovated, rather than demolished like the majority of its neighbours. It would be nice to think that this unlikely survivor at 116 Forest Heights Boulevard points the way to a new appreciation of the area's remaining historic properties.

Chapter Twelve

The Cummers

It is doubtful that any pioneer family had a greater impact on North York than the Cummers. The Kummer family, as they were known in their native Germany (some sources also list their names as Koomer), began the remarkable journey that would eventually lead them to Willowdale when they sailed to North America in the mid-1700s to escape religious persecution in their home country. The Kummers were Lutherans, a denomination that had long been at odds with the Catholic Church and many of the Crown heads of Europe.

They left their home in the Palatine region of southwestern Germany, where Martin Luther had started the Reformation in 1517, to settle in Pennsylvania in 1736. The family was welcomed in those prerevolutionary days when Britain still governed their colonies south of the border. It was only natural then that the family felt a certain loyalty to Great Britain, and, although they remained in the United States for some time after the Revolutionary War of 1776, they eventually felt the pull of the British Crown and decided to move north of the border.

Jacob Kummer was born in Reading, Pennsylvania, in 1767, three years before Beethoven. He became one of the first settlers in North York when he emigrated with his wife

Elizabeth, the first three of their thirteen children, Mary, Elizabeth, and Daniel, his father Daniel, and Elizabeth's father Jacob Fisher in 1795. Upon arriving in Upper Canada, they built a little log cabin near present-day Yonge and Eglinton, where Jacob left the rest of the family for the winter while he continued north into the wilderness to seek a more permanent home. Their son John was born in the cabin in 1797.

That same year the Kummers received their first Crown land grant for the one-hundred-and-ninety-acre Lot 18-1E halfway between Sheppard and Finch, running from Yonge Street east to Bayview. Not all lots in North York were exactly two hundred acres, owing to surveying mistakes. Jacob had carefully selected this particular lot for its combination of hard and softwood trees, as well as its excellent soil and gently rolling terrain. The family performed their settlers' duties to the Crown's satisfaction, including the building of another log cabin on Yonge Street, and were granted the deed to their property before the nineteenth century, one of only a handful of families who were able to make that claim.

To give some idea of just how isolated the Kummers were, it should be mentioned that there were only three neighbours in a four-mile radius around their farm. In 1797, there were only 241 people in the town of York, as well as 175 soldiers and family members at Fort York, and 196 settlers in the surrounding countryside for a grand total of 612 people in the present-day city of Toronto. They all could have fit into three subway cars. Outside, in the Toronto of 1797, bears, wolves, and foxes were a constant threat to crops and livestock.

One day when Elizabeth Kummer was home alone tending to her chores and her newborn son, John, she was startled by a Native man staring at her through the door of the cabin. He appeared to be interested in a kitchen knife that was sitting on the table. She gave him the knife, hoping he would go away and leave her in peace. He accepted the knife and went on his way. Relieved, Elizabeth went back to her chores and put the matter out of her mind. Some days later, however, the man appeared again, bearing a cradle that he had made for the baby to thank Elizabeth for the knife. He had come all the way from his home on Lake Simcoe. Perhaps he had also been taken by the very appearance of this baby, who was thought to be the first white child born in the wilderness north of Toronto. This would be the first of many happy interactions between the family and the First Nations people who still lived in the area.

More children would come in fairly rapid succession: Katherine in 1798, Jacob II in 1800, David in 1803, and Joseph in 1804. As the family grew, so too did their holdings. Even their family name would change, but more on that later.

In 1804, Jacob bought the southern ninety-five acres of the adjoining farm to the north, on Lot 19-1E, from fellow settler Lawrence Johnson. In 1817, he expanded the family's reach in a northeasterly direction when he bought fifty acres in the centre of Lot 22-2E, a two-hundred-acre parcel bordered on the north by today's Cummer Avenue, stretching from Bayview to Leslie Street. Two years later he would add the western hundred acres of Lot 21-2E directly to the south, and

in 1821 he would add the one-hundred-and-ninety-acre Lot 23-1E, north of Cummer Avenue, running from Yonge Street east to Bayview Avenue.

Jacob Kummer now had an unbroken one-hundred-and-fifty-acre parcel between Bayview and Leslie, as well as a two-hundred-and-eighty-five-acre farm between Yonge Street and Bayview, and a one-hundred-and-ninety-acre farm further north, also stretching from Yonge to Bayview. By now the family was complete, with daughters Sarah and Nancy and sons Joshua and Samuel joining their elder siblings between 1804 and 1815. Some years after Samuel's birth in 1815, the family would change their name to "Cummer." Sadly, two other children would not live to see adulthood — Joseph living only from 1804 to 1813 and Peter dying the same year as Joseph at the age of one.

The family's holdings now stood at a most impressive six-hundred-and-twenty-five acres, only twenty-four years removed from that first cabin at Yonge and Eglinton. The Yonge Street and Don Valley properties would serve different yet complementary purposes. Yonge Street was Upper Canada's main street at the time, offering unequalled contact with other settlers and relatively quick transportation of farm products to market. The Don River, on the other hand, offered the valuable advantage of water power.

While it's true that the headwaters of Wilket Creek rose on the Kummers' Yonge Street property, the flow was insufficient to power any significant sort of mill and in pioneer Upper Canada, a mill could shift a man from being a "mere" farmer to the more exalted realm of merchant, for now he would be able to process his own goods for sale, as well as his neighbours' goods for profit. The East Don River ran right through the middle of the Kummers' more easterly holdings and had more than enough water flow to power any sort of mill. It was here on the banks of the Don River that the Kummers made their stand and left one of the only traces of their built history that survives to the present day. In 1819, the family opened a sawmill on the East Don River, where Cummer Avenue crosses the river today, west of Leslie Street. The sawmill was operated by Jacob's son John, but the mill site would soon have value far beyond its commercial activities.

Jacob Kummer was a devout Lutheran. It has been said that his courage was rooted in his faith. Sadly for him, Lutherans were uncommon in early Upper Canada. There was a strong Methodist presence, however, and this is where Jacob elected to shift his loyalties, joining a number of his children who had already become Episcopal Methodists. The Kummer property on the Don River soon became known far and wide for the church services and camp meetings that were held there. Such was the influence of these activities that First Nations tribes from as far away as Lake Simcoe were regular participants. At the time, early settlers and Natives got along well, to the point of inter-marrying without any apparent stigma on either side.

The product of one such union was the Reverend Peter Jones, a Wesleyan missionary who was also part Native. He was the second son of the deputy provincial surveyor, Augustus Jones, who had helped Lieutenant Governor John Graves Simcoe in the construction of Yonge Street in the 1790s, and Tuhbenahneequay, daughter of Mississauga Chief Wahbanosay of Burlington Bay, where the city of Hamilton stands today. Reverend Jones presided at one particular camp meeting on the Cummer property in the summer of 1826 where he noted that "a number of both whites and Indians professed to experience a change of heart, at the close, several Indians received the solemn ordinance of baptism."[1]

It was not uncommon for several hundred First Nations people from the areas around Lake Simcoe and Lake Scugog to attend the meetings. At such times, the campground was ringed with board tents, including one massive tent that mea-sured 240 feet by 15 feet and was built to simulate a Native longhouse, so that the visitors could arrange themselves in family groups within the tent and feel more comfortable while away from home. Other smaller tents were provided for other visitors. The tents featured board roofs, not surprising at a sawmill site, and sides made of boards and brush. Meetings typically lasted several days and continued well into the mid-1800s, by which time they featured upwards of thirty tents and up to half-a-dozen ministers. So popular and well-known were the meetings that the area came to be known as "Scripture Town" and later as "Angel Valley."

The area where the campground once stood is still visible in a relatively un-altered state where Cummer Avenue crosses the East Don River, halfway between Bayview and Leslie. Cummer Avenue was originally the wagon trail that the family laid out to connect their Yonge Street farms to the mill property in the Don Valley. The Don River itself is sadly diminished from pioneer days. An article on the Cummers in *The Willowdale Enterprise* of June 18, 1953, describes the river at that time as "an insignificant stream." Look to the current size of the *valley* to get a rough idea of how large and powerful the river must have been when it was young.

As the Kummer children grew up, they also began to acquire land in the area. John Kummer, who had been the lucky recipient of the hand-made cradle, was the most acquisitive. In 1819, the same year he began to run his father's sawmill, John bought the two-hundred-and-ten acre Lot 21-1W, the first farm north of Finch, between Yonge Street and Bathurst Street. In 1831 he bought the northern one-hundred-and-five acres of Lot 18-1W, adjoining David Gibson's farm on the south half of the same lot. Between 1835 and 1840, John bought the two-hundred-acre Lot 24-2E and the western one hundred acres of Lot 23-2E, directly north of the campgrounds on the East Don River, bringing the family's holdings in the Don Valley to four-hundred-and-fifty acres and their Yonge Street properties to seven-hundred-and-ninety acres. John's brother, Jacob II, would expand the family's holdings to over 1,300 acres when he bought the northern eighty acres of Lot 21-2E near the northeast corner of Yonge and Finch in 1854. The family's activities on their Yonge Street farms would prove every bit as influential as what they accomplished at the mill site and campground.

Jacob Kummer was a well-informed man who was accomplished in a dizzying array of disciplines. He was a blacksmith, a carpenter, a stonemason, tool-maker, shingle-maker, wagon-maker, inventor, and insurance agent. Not only did he make his own tools, he opened a shop where he made the tools available to his neighbours. The shop on Yonge Street became such a focal point of local activity that Willowdale was originally known as Kummer's Settlement, and Jacob was thought of as a politician without an office.[2] He became known as the area's unofficial peacemaker. The other early farmers were grateful to have such a skilled individual from whom to obtain their ploughs, scythes, cradles, sleighs, and wagons. One implement in particular, the Kummer Plough, was so popular that Jacob patented it and struggled to manufacture enough to keep up with the demand. Jacob employed peddlers to carry the store's wares to those who were unable to come to the store and he would often work for his neighbours without compensation. He also served as the local veterinarian and in a pinch would treat human patients as well, this at a time when bleeding was still an accepted treatment for a number of ailments.

The Kummers' farms were as perfect as any farm could be — clean, organized, and strict. Barns, stables, yards, and houses were exceedingly well kept. Jacob's grain bags were made at home from flax and stamped with the initials "JK," as was the wood from his sawmill. Jacob had a good constitution and a strong faith. He was temperate and never idle. No portrait of Jacob exists, as he lived in a time before photography and was probably too busy or just not interested in sitting still for a portrait.

At home, Elizabeth and Jacob spoke German to each other as well as English. The children spoke mostly English and eventually the use of the German language faded away. The when and why of the family's name change is unclear. It seems likely it had a practical purpose since the family was already so well-respected in the community that they wouldn't have had to Anglicize their name just to fit in. One family remembrance suggests that it was much easier to stamp "JC" than "JK" on the grain bags and wooden boards from the sawmill, and this is why Jacob made the change. Jacob's daughter-in-law, Angelina, said the name was changed when her husband Joshua was a boy. As Joshua and Angelina were married in 1835, and Joshua was born in 1810, the family became the Cummers, sometime around 1820.

The Cummers' religious involvement extended to Yonge Street as well. In 1834, Jacob donated half an acre on Yonge Street for the construction of a new church on what would one day be the north-east corner of Yonge Street and Church Avenue. Lawrence Johnson, one of the few people to settle in North York before Jacob Cummer, donated an adjoining parcel for a cemetery. Jacob, not content with merely donating the land, built the new log Episcopal Methodist meeting house virtually by himself. In 1856, some years after Jacob's death, when the congregation had outgrown the meeting house, the Cummer and Johnson families got together again to build a new brick church.

Jacob's son Samuel built the impressive spire, which became a landmark visible for miles around. It stood for three-quarters of a century before being toppled by a violent wind storm in the mid-1920s. The church itself suffered the indignity of having its "face" cut off to allow for the widening of Yonge Street in 1931. A number of graves were expropriated at this time as well, with some of the interred being personally reburied elsewhere by disgruntled family members.

Photo by Ted Chirnside, Toronto Public Library, TC 38.

John Cummer's house, on the northwest corner of Yonge and Finch, had more than enough to recommend it for preservation when it was dismantled in 1959 — four years after this photo was taken. Built in 1819, with a verandah across the front, it was the scene of John's capture by government troops on the night of December 8, 1837, after they mistakenly identified him as a participant in the Upper Canada Rebellion. While the house then gave shelter to Eliza Gibson and her children as her husband David fled for his life from the pursuing troops, it would find no shelter of its own from the grasping tentacles of a relentlessly growing city.

Another new church was built on Kenneth Avenue in 1954. The old church was demolished on the autumn equinox in 1956. A scattering of forgotten pioneer headstones were shuffled around like a cheap deck of cards and left, cracked and deteriorating on the ground when Yonge Street was further altered and expanded in the late 1970s, where they remain to this day, near an emergency exit for the subway, behind a grocery store. Jacob Cummer's headstone fared a little better, being incorporated into a newer monument in the middle of this sad little cemetery.

Also lying on the ground is a stone that reads, "United Church of Canada 1932," nearly one hundred years after Jacob built the log meeting house with his own two hands. The little log meeting house also played a part in the Upper Canada Rebellion. It seems that the Cummers, like the Harrisons of York Mills, made the decision to turn their backs on their Loyalist roots when they began to feel that Upper Canada's ruling Family Compact was ignoring the farmers' legitimate concerns.

The Family Compact, a clique of privileged and inter-related families, rose to power by championing popular government, but once in office, their goal changed to simply maintaining their authority. Once they had gained control by making popular decisions, they became arrogant and began to make many unpopular decisions. Included among these was their decision to reserve 2,500,000 acres of Crown land for the exclusive use of the Anglican Church. Other denominations felt excluded and offended. The disgruntled farmers decided that the best way to deal with this problem was head-on, so they formed the Reform Party, which had slowly but surely taken control of Upper Canada's Legislative Assembly or lower house by 1834. Still, the Family Compact, who controlled the upper house, refused to make legislative changes.

John Cummer, the first member of his family to be born in Upper Canada, was elected to the Legislative Assembly as a Reformer in 1834, as was his neighbour David Gibson. John, like party leader and close friend William Lyon Mackenzie, wanted to give a voice to the farmers who were fed up with corrupt politicians, land speculators, and administrative extravagance, but even though the Reformers now controlled the lower house, the Family Compact was not really interested in listening to their concerns.

A number of the Cummer brothers and their fellow Reformers gathered to pray at the little meeting house on December 4, 1837, the day the Rebellion began, to seek divine guidance. The Cummers, who were not prone to violent or treasonable acts, decided not to join the Rebellion, despite John Cummer being offered the outright command of the rebel forces by rebel leader William Lyon Mackenzie. As was seen in the story of the Montgomery/Elliot farm, the Rebellion itself was a failure in name only, for although the rag-tag group of farmers with their pitchforks and clubs were easily dispatched by the well-armed government troops, their concerns would be addressed and the rebels were eventually pardoned and allowed to return to their farms. Shortly afterwards, the government *did* change to address the farmers' concerns, and create a template for today's government.

Among those arrested in the days immediately following the Rebellion were John Cummer and his younger brother Samuel. John was arrested on December 8 at his home at Yonge and Finch. Although he had not participated in the Rebellion, government troops had observed him looking at the remains of his friend David Gibson's house, which had been burned by the troops the previous night. This was reason enough for them to ride their horses up onto John's verandah and take him into custody in front of his terrified wife and children.

Courtesy of North York Historical Society, NYHS 1327.

This view of Jacob Cummer III's house is no longer obtainable, as two houses have been built in front of it since this shot was taken by Lorna Gardner in 1967. This is a significant photograph that allows us to easily visualize the way the house looked before the two wings were added in 1930.

John Cummer was roped to other captured Reformers, marched down Yonge Street in front of a jeering mob, and incarcerated in the Toronto jail on the north side of King Street, across from today's King Edward Hotel. Luckily for John, he had Family Compact friends in the Legislative Assembly, such as his brother-in-law Peter Lawrence, who was married to his older sister Elizabeth, and business associates such as Sir Allan Napier MacNab, a prominent Markham distiller and dedicated customer of John's sawmill, who made sure that he only spent one night in jail. In fact, Sir Allan owed John quite a bit of money at this time, so maybe he had mixed motives. John's younger brother Samuel was also jailed, and, in fact, forcibly drafted into the government army before being cut loose the next morning when it occurred to someone in charge that he was too young to serve. Jacob's son Joshua hid William Lyon Mackenzie's printing press in an abandoned well on his farm so that the Reform Party could continue printing their newspaper, *The Colonial Advocate*. John Cummer and his family offered refuge to David Gibson's wife, Eliza, and the four Gibson children after their house was destroyed.

Jacob Cummer died suddenly on December 5, 1841, at seventy-four years of age. And, yes, he had outlived Beethoven. For many years after his death, the community that came to be known as Willowdale continued to be referred to as Cummer's Settlement. Jacob had led an incredible life and done his best to ensure that his children would be able to do the same. It had been his custom to give land to his sons as wedding gifts, just as many other settlers did. Jacob had executed his own will in 1834 and it showed that he played no favourites. All of his children were remembered: John inherited the sawmill that he had been running for twenty-two years, Joshua was given the deed to the north half of the original family farms on Yonge Street, and Samuel inherited the southern half. Jacob was buried in the cemetery on Yonge Street, next to the church that he built with his own two hands. In his will he specified that the church remain available to all denominations "forever." Although nothing lasts forever, this little meeting house and the brick church that replaced it would become the spiritual birthplace of the United Church of Canada, which brought the Methodists, Congregationalists, and some groups of Presbyterians together under one roof when incorporated in 1925. Maybe Jacob got his wish after all.

Elizabeth survived her husband by a little over twelve years, living with her son Joshua and his wife Angelina Irwin. One of her grandchildren offered this memory of Elizabeth, as quoted by Gladys Allison in the the *Willowdale Enterprise* of June 18, 1953: "She attended to the moral and other affairs of the daily routine and used what was handiest in the due repression of any evil doing or intent on the part of the large family which looked to her as captain and helmsman." She was kindly yet masterful and when she died on her seventy-ninth birthday on March 31, 1854, she handed the reins to the next generation of Cummers — the first generation to be born in North America, and a generation that must have been a source of great pride for Jacob and Elizabeth.

As in most families, some of the children would go on to have more of an impact on their community than others, and, with ten of them surviving their parents and marrying members of other prominent pioneer families, there is more to tell than is possible here.

Of all the members of the second generation, it was John, the first Cummer born in Upper Canada, who was the most dedicated farmer. His holdings would ultimately exceed six hundred acres at their peak, including a three-hundred-acre farm just north of the camp-meeting grounds on the Don River, a two-hundred-and-ten-acre farm that ran from Yonge Street to Bathurst Street on the north side of Finch Avenue, and a 105-acre farm that ran from Yonge to Bathurst, just north of the David Gibson farm, between Sheppard and Finch. An inventory of this latter farm from the 1830s showed the following commodities being produced: wheat, peas, oats, potatoes, hay, maple sugar, cider, apples, wool, cheese, milk, butter, pork, and beef. This was truly a well-balanced farm that would have been able to withstand market-value fluctuations by being so diverse. When the lumber from John's sawmill on the Don River was added to this mix, there was an almost perfect combination of marketable products. Only a couple of things were missing and they would be seen to in good time.

Photo by Scott Kennedy

The house that Samuel Cummer built facing Yonge Street, around 1840, is shown here, one hundred years after it was moved to 48 Parkview Avenue in 1913.

In 1851, ten years after his father's death, John and his son, Jacob III, added a gristmill and a woollen mill to the family holdings in the Don Valley, near the meeting grounds. The gristmill was located near the sawmill and meeting grounds, while the woollen mill was further south along the river. They named their cluster of mills "Reading Mills" after the family's former home in Pennsylvania. At the same time they were building the new mills, Jacob III was building one of the only two Cummer homes to survive to the present day.

Currently located at 44 Beardmore Crescent, in the valley just north of Cummer Avenue, the house originally consisted of only the centre section of the structure that exists today. The wings on either side were added in 1930 by Henry Nathanson, who owned the house at that time and used it as a summer residence to escape the heat and congestion of a still-distant Toronto.

As already noted, John's brothers, Joshua and Samuel, each inherited one half of their father Jacob's original farms on Lot 18-1E and Lot 19-1E. Joshua was a tinsmith. He sold his wares, as well as the shingles from his shingle mill, at the Cummer store on Yonge Street. In the 1830s he built a house there that stood at 20 McKee Avenue until the twenty-first century. The farm and house had been sold by Joshua to John Morgan for $15,000 in 1876, when Joshua moved to Aurora. John Morgan sold the property to John Arnold McKee in 1910. The property remained part of the McKee's Hildon Farm until John Arnold's son, John William, sold the land for development in 1923. Throughout, the house survived. But concerted conservation efforts at the dawn of the twenty-first century failed to save the house, which was still in fine shape when it was mindlessly demolished in June of 2002 for condos.

In 1856, Samuel Cummer helped to build the new brick church on Yonge Street that replaced the original log meeting house his father had built in 1834. The new place of wor-

ship stood on Yonge for one hundred years until it too was consigned to the scrap heap in 1956. Samuel also served as Willowdale postmaster from 1880–82. The brick farmhouse that Samuel built around 1840 still stands at 48 Parkview Avenue, several doors east of its original location at 34 Parkview Avenue; an address that is now home to the Ontario Historical Society. Though altered considerably and now divided into two houses, Samuel's is one of only two remaining Cummer houses in Willowdale.

Samuel's brother Jacob II, the first Willowdale postmaster, had taken the store over from his father and ran the post office there from 1855 until 1880 when Samuel assumed the position. Jacob II was also a tinsmith and shingle-maker, and he and his wife, the former Agnes Endicott, were much admired in the community for taking in numerous orphaned boys and girls who were then educated and treated exactly like their own children until they were able to make their way in the world.

Brothers David and Daniel were active in the Temperance movement. Both men occupied the Cummer house that is pictured on the east side of Yonge Street, facing Patricia Avenue, although they lived there at different times. Their older sister Katherine also lived in the house for many years with her husband, Elihu Pease. The house was demolished in 1964, and, unlike current demolitions where everything goes into the dumpster, some comfort can be taken from the fact that this house was carefully dismantled in the old-fashioned way, allowing the building materials to be used again.

In the latter part of the nineteenth century, a strange thing began to happen — the Cummers started leaving North York. Not all of them, but enough that their influence began to wane. Their farms were sold to new families and remained productive until the late 1950s.

Photo by A.J. Tilton, North York Historical Society, NYHS 437.

Despite the almost delicate appearance of the frame construction in this demolition photo from April 1964, this house served the Cummers well, and stood its ground at 6059 Yonge Street for 145 years. It is shown, vacant and awaiting demolition, but still in one piece in the chapter (3) on Elihu Pease.

John Cummer was the first to go. Even before he built the mills in the Don Valley with his son Jacob III, he had sent another son, Lockman Abram Cummer, to supervise the construction of a new house in Waterdown, Ontario. It seems that John had contracted cholera following the Upper Canada Rebellion, and, although he recovered, health concerns dictated the move to the less-populous Waterdown. The house

there was completed by 1848 and still stands at 265 Mill Street South. Lockman liked the town so much that he stayed there after the house was finished and married Rachel Lottridge, the daughter of a local businessman.

Shortly after the Cummers completed their new Don Valley mills, John, Lockman, and their new partner, William Gill, built a flour mill in Waterdown. They also opened an iron foundry to produce millstones, boilers, and steam engines in the aptly named Smokey Hollow just outside of Waterdown. The partnership was short-lived however, as depressed grain markets caused them to close the mill in 1857. The foundry was also sold and the partnership was dissolved. John moved from Waterdown to the United States to "take advantage" of opportunities created by the American Civil War. He remained there until 1863 when he returned to Waterdown and partnered in a new venture with his son's in-laws, the Lottridges.

John Cummer, the first white person to be born north of the town of York, died at his son Franklin's house in Toronto on September 11, 1868. His wife Sarah died of paralysis in Waterdown on April 13, 1870. Their son, Jacob III, sold the woollen mill and moved to Cadillac, Michigan, in 1860. Their children, those who remained in North York, continued to operate the family businesses for several more years. John and Sarah's son William took over his grandfather Jacob's store on Yonge Street from his uncle, Jacob II, in 1867, leaving the milling to his brothers Albert and Edwin. In 1878, the mills were sold to James Cooper. One has to feel for Mr. Cooper, since 1878 was the year that virtually all mills on both branches of the Don River were wiped out by a massive flood that crested for three days, from September 10 to September 13.

John's brother Joshua sold his portion of the original farm on Yonge Street in 1876 and moved to Aurora, where he died in 1879. Brother Daniel moved to Waterloo in 1847 and to Niagara Township in 1856. He died in 1882. Brother Samuel Cummer died in June 1883 on the Yonge Street farm where he had been born sixty-eight years earlier. He had been deeply involved in his community, especially with the Methodist Episcopal Church, and his passing was mourned by all. Sister Katherine, who had been married to Elihu Pease for many years, died in 1886 at the age of eighty-eight. She was the last of Jacob and Elizabeth Cummer's children

and her death brought an end to the second generation of the Cummer family in Canada. Three years later, the last of the Cummers' land was sold when Samuel's son, George W. Cummer, sold the southern half of his grandfather's original land grant to a Harriet E. Flook.

In a little over fifty years, the Cummers took over 1,300 acres of wilderness, cleared enough of it to create half a dozen farms, built roads, churches, mills, and stores, filled the stores with products that they made themselves, formed meaningful bonds with the Native people, held political office, fought for the rights of their fellow farmers, and sowed the seeds for the United Church of Canada.

What remains of their legacy? Well, not quite everything they built has been torn down *yet*. There is still the Samuel Cummer house on Parkview Avenue, and that one last house on Beardmore Crescent, way down there in Angel Valley — not much, but much better than nothing.

Chapter Thirteen

The David Gibson Farm

For someone with less than two hundred acres of farmland, David Gibson certainly made his presence known, not only in North York but throughout Upper Canada. His name crops up frequently, since he interacts with many of the more notable families of early North York. His name often appears in the present day as well, for he was the man who built Gibson House at Yonge Street and Park Home Avenue, arguably the most accurately restored and maintained pioneer farmhouse in all of North York. Though currently being dwarfed by the construction of yet another high-rise development, to be named Gibson Square, of course, one needs only to step over the threshold to forget such intrusions and become absorbed into the lives that were once lived here. Gibson House is, in fact, the second house the family built on the property, the first having been burned by government troops following the Upper Canada Rebellion in 1837.

The only child of tenant farmer James Gibson and his wife Margaret, David was born in the parish of Glamis, Forfarshire, Scotland, on March 9, 1804. His uncle, Alexander Milne, also born in Forfarshire in 1777, had immigrated to the United States in 1801, and made considerable money working as a weaver and running a woollen mill, as well as patenting and popularizing a new method of bleaching cotton, before coming to Upper Canada in 1817. David's mother died in 1811. His father married Isobel Cathow around eight years later, and they would have four more children together: James Junior, William, John, and Isabella.

When David Gibson was still a young boy, William Blackadder, a surveyor working near the Gibson home, asked for the boy's assistance. David must have acquitted himself well, for when the survey was completed, Blackadder asked if David might train as his apprentice. James Gibson agreed and David spent the next five years learning the surveyor's trade. David's apprenticeship, begun in 1819, was completed by June 1824. Armed with his new credentials and letters of recommendation, David set sail from Dundee on the brigantine *Gratitude* on March 28, 1825, bound for Canada.

By May he was settled in Quebec City where he was received by the surveyor general of Quebec who sent him with one other surveyor and four Native guides to survey the headwaters of the Saint John River, which rise in what is now

The Gibson House Museum in restored condition, as it looked in 2010, snuggled among the same pine trees that have kept it company since before Canada was a country.

Photo by Scott Kennedy.

the state of Maine. For thirty-two days they travelled on foot, crossing lakes on homemade rafts, and living on rations of bread, salt pork, peas, and whatever fish or partridges they could catch. When that job was completed, David found a position with a crew who were surveying the border between the United States and Quebec. He worked in Quebec until

the end of September, then decided to head west to seek out his uncles, Alexander and Peter Milne, in the autumn of 1825. By then they were the proprietors of a sawmill, a grist-mill, a woollen mill, and a dry goods store in Markham Township, in the area then known as Markham Mills, at the corner of present-day Highways 7 and 48.

Leaving snow-covered Montreal in late October, David travelled night and day to reach Kingston, but once there he discovered that there were no schooners or stagecoaches heading to York, so he continued on foot. He recalled the journey in a letter to a friend back in Scotland, dated April 27, 1827:

> I put a clean shirt and pair of stockings in my pocket and six days afterwards I arrived in the Township of Markham about eighteen miles north east of York in U. Canada where I was kindly received by my friends. They wrote me when in Quebec to come to Upper Canada, that they had no doubt that I would get plenty of employment, and gave me great encouragement. My friends were very glad to see the letters I had with me from the Governor of Lower Canada. I went to York a few days after and delivered my Introductory Letters, the one was to the Rev. Dr. Strachan and the other to the Lieut. Governor, they both advised me to get appointed a Deputy Surveyor of Land. I was examined by the Surveyor General, found competent and got a commission written out in the usual form signed by the Lieut. Governor (after I found security in the amount of £500 for my good behaviour, my friends in Markham were my securities) the Lieut. Governor gave me back Lord Dalhousie's letter and stated that there was no situation vacant then but as soon as I saw a situation vacant that I would like to apply for it and again show Lord Dalhousie's letter. Since I was appointed a Deputy Surveyor I petitioned the Magistrates of the Home District to appoint me a Surveyor of Highways of the Home District which they granted, the clerk of the quarter Sessions then stated to the Magistrates that the Surveyor of Highways for the Eastern division of the Home District was a very illiterate sort of man and that they never got a proper report from him and also asked if they would have any objection to appoint me for the Eastern Division also which they readily granted since I have been appointed Surveyor of Highways for the Southern division of the Home District I have as much business as I can attend to.[1]

David used the time between December 28, 1825, when he was commissioned as a surveyor for Upper Canada, and the spring of 1826 when given his actual appointments, to get his surveying equipment in order, a task that involved cutting the rings for his surveying chain, linking the chain together, grinding the glass in his surveying instruments, and calibrating the instruments by finding a true Meridian Line from the stars. The Gibson family still has David's original chain.

The scope of his appointments, all made in May 1826, was almost unbelievable. Under David Gibson's direction, colonization roads were built from as far east as Whitby to as far west as Southampton on Lake Huron, and north to Owen Sound on Georgian Bay. He surveyed much of Simcoe, Grey, Huron, and Bruce Counties as well as townships in Wellington and Wentworth Counties, and those for the future Dufferin County. He was later put in charge of surveying the roads in the Algoma District, all this at a time when these areas were complete wilderness. After all, until someone laid out the colonization roads, there could be no settlers.

Courtesy of the City of Toronto and the Gibson House Museum.

This portrait of David Gibson, dated circa 1855, is on display in Gibson House Museum.

A photograph of Eliza Gibson hangs beside the photo of her husband David. Her picture is believed to have been taken about fifteen years later.

On March 4, 1828, David took time out from his labours to get married. His bride was his cousin, Eliza Milne, daughter of Alexander, who was then operating a mill where Toronto's Edwards Gardens stands today. The newlyweds built their first house on the Milne property at Leslie and Lawrence. The following year, David and Eliza purchased the southern half of Lot 18-1W from John Willson III for £400 and settled down to the business of farming. Their new frame house stood on the same spot where the current Gibson house stands today. The farm property, the southern one hundred and five acres of Lot 18-1W, ran west from today's Yonge Street to Bathurst Street, about halfway between Sheppard and Finch Avenues.

Much of the land was already cleared. It had been granted, in 1805, to John Willson II, who had fought with the British during the American Revolution, and had remained in the Willson family for twenty-four years. Following the war, the Willsons had been forced to flee to New Brunswick after their property south of the border was confiscated. They arrived in Upper Canada at the end of the eighteenth century and were among the most prominent of the early families in North York, eventually giving their slightly modified name to Wilson Avenue.

In 1833, David Gibson acquired some additional property, the eastern fifty acres of Lot 16-1E, on the northwest corner of Sheppard and Bayview Avenues. The Gibson family would continue to acquire portions of this lot, eventually owning ninety-six acres (as well as a ten-acre portion of Lot 16-2E) by the end of the nineteenth century, which brought their total land holdings to two hundred and eleven acres. By now the Gibson family was growing, with Elizabeth born in 1829, James in 1831, and William in 1833. Five more children would follow: David, born 1835 (died 1836); Peter Silas, born in 1837; Margaret, in 1840; George, in1842; and Elizabeth Mary, in 1844.

It might seem that starting a family, running two farms, and surveying much of southern Ontario would be enough to keep a man occupied, but David Gibson thought otherwise. In 1831, he was elected president of the local Temperance Society. He also found himself among the growing number of local farmers who were fed up with the way that the ruling Family Compact continued to fill their own pockets while treating the farmers' concerns with disdain. So David threw his hat into the political ring.

In September 1834, he was nominated as a candidate for the Legislative Assembly of Upper Canada, representing the Reform Party. He was nominated at Thomas Sheppard's Golden Lion Inn, along with John Cummer, James Davis, Joseph Shepard II, and James Hogg. The new party elected William Lyon Mackenzie as its leader, primarily because he was the only Reformer in the area who owned a printing press. Mackenzie was also elected as Toronto's first mayor in 1834, the year that York became Toronto.

By the 1830s, the Reform Party was gaining considerable strength, especially in the outlying rural areas. David Gibson was elected to the Legislative Assembly in 1834 and 1836. In fact, the party elected so many members that, by 1837, Reformers actually controlled the Legislative Assembly, the lower house of Upper Canada's government. The problem was that the Family Compact, who still controlled the upper house, continued to dismiss the farmers' concerns. In 1835, the Legislative Assembly sent William Lyon Mackenzie to London, England, bearing a petition signed by 24,500 Upper Canadians asking the King to address their concerns. Even this plea from the overwhelming majority of citizens failed to bring about any sort of change. Having done their best to play by the rules, the farmers began to believe that their only recourse lay in a much more direct form of opposition.

Many Reformers now felt that physical force was the only tool left to engage the Family Compact. In 1837, groups of militia began training at the Shepard family's mill site near present-day Bathurst and Sheppard, and also on the Gibson farm. David Gibson was appointed controller of the military organization of the rebels. As many as two hundred men would train at a time, trying to determine the most effective ways to use their numbers and their limited weapons, which were mostly simple farm implements and the occasional musket, to launch a successful overthrow of the upper house. The men came from the immediate vicinity and from many miles away, taking precious time away from the never-ending farm work in an attempt to ensure better lives for themselves and their families. As autumn settled in on Upper Canada and the harvest drew to a close, training intensified and resolve strengthened.

Thursday, December 7, 1837, was chosen as the date the Reformers would march south on Yonge Street to engage the government's loyalist soldiers, but as the day grew near, farmers to the north became a little over-eager. It seems that they had been told that Toronto was currently undefended, so they jumped the gun and headed south. Travelling on foot through the snow-covered countryside, 150 "soldiers" arrived at Montgomery's Tavern on Sunday, December 3. The tavern had been selected as a staging area because of the incredibly strategic view it commanded of the surrounding countryside from its location on the hill at present-day Yonge Street and Broadway Avenue. Though hard to believe, in today's high-rise world, it was once possible to see both Lake Ontario and the heights of the Oak Ridges Moraine from the tavern's upper floor.

The tavern, however, only had accommodations for two-thirds of the men. The situation grew tense as the farmers, by now quite tired, cold, and hungry, were reduced to commandeering food from local Reform supporters. By Tuesday, December 5, a large group of them had grown so impatient that they grabbed their weapons and headed out on their own. Quickly defeated by the government's superior firepower, they retreated to Montgomery's Tavern. One rebel had been killed, allegedly by a stray bullet, but the Reformers had somehow been able to take a number of loyalist prisoners. Apparently, the zealous Reformers had caught their foes somewhat by surprise, for even as they retreated to the tavern, word came that more troops were arriving from the east and west. On Wednesday, both sides regrouped. By Thursday, it was all over.

Early Thursday morning, one thousand government soldiers advanced up Yonge Street, armed with muskets and two cannons. The three or four hundred rebels were not only severely out-gunned and out-numbered; they had also been surprised by the early morning attack. For some idea of just

how ill-equipped the rebels were, one need not look any further than their leader, William Lyon Mackenzie, who wore several overcoats as he went into battle — his own personal armour. Only 150 rebels had muskets, and they stationed themselves near the fence fronting the tavern. The others, armed with pitchforks and clubs, hung back by the walls of the tavern. The encounter was brief, lasting no more than fifteen or twenty minutes.

The first cannonball ripped through the walls of an adjoining tavern, the second through the walls of the rebel stronghold. Musket fire was exchanged, and, as the unarmed rebels fled into the surrounding fields and woods, Lieutenant Governor Sir Francis Bond Head ordered Montgomery's Tavern burned to the ground, declaring that the tavern's destruction would signal the death of "that perfidious enemy, responsible government."[2]

The resulting fire was so intense that William Gray, who was grinding flour at his mill over five miles away, near the corner of Don Mills Road and York Mills Road, saw the burning embers of the tavern as the wind carried them over his mill. Casualties were surprisingly few — one rebel killed, eleven rebels wounded (four of whom would later die in hospital), one loyalist killed, and five loyalists wounded. David Gibson, who had been in charge of the loyalist prisoners at the tavern, had marched his prisoners north along Yonge Street to protect them from the gunfire. As government troops pursued him, he turned his prisoners loose around today's Lawrence Park and ran for his own life.

On the direct orders of the lieutenant governor, Sir Francis Bond Head, de facto head of the Family Compact, government soldiers continued north on Yonge Street and set fire to the Gibson house and barns. Eliza fled into the winter night with her four children, leaving baby Peter Silas Gibson in a snowbank with his siblings standing guard while she ran back into the house to save some of her husband's surveying equipment and the workings and face of a prized grandfather clock. She then found refuge in a nearby parsonage before being taken in by neighbour John Cummer. The Gibsons' hired hands had the presence of mind to set the horses free, allowing them to flee into the woods at the west end of the farm. The pigs and chickens weren't so lucky. The government soldiers slaughtered them all, and rode away with the carcasses.

David, meanwhile, fled southeast through the biting December cold, not stopping until he reached the safety of his cousin William Milne's house in Milneford Mills, where Lawrence Avenue East crosses the East Don River. William was Alexander Milne's eldest son, and, though he wasn't running from the government troops, his brother Peter was. Peter and David were hidden in a woodpile behind the family's sawmill until a fellow rebel came to spirit David away. The two men then headed east where David found sanctuary at a friend's farm near Oshawa. He stayed there until mid-January of the following year, hiding himself from the government troops by burrowing his way into a haystack. Though soldiers searched the farm several times and plunged their swords into all of the haystacks, David somehow avoided detection. By now, there was a bounty on his head of £500, ironically the same amount he had been granted by the former lieutenant governor for "good behaviour," just twelve years earlier. Peter Milne was eventually captured, but was released after his trial, on bond for good behaviour.

In mid-January 1838, David Gibson and a number of his fellow rebels, all of whom had been indicted for high treason, fled into exile in the United States, crossing Lake Ontario in a small, open boat. Landing on the other side of the lake in Rochester, New York, with little more than the clothes on his back, David found a surprisingly warm welcome, and, in short order, some employment.

Leaving her children with members of the Cummer family, Eliza made a brief journey to Rochester, bringing her husband's tools, clothes, and £180. On the basis of his impressive credentials, and, with the assistance of an influential friend or two, David was soon working on major projects such as the expansion of the Erie Canal, where he was hired as first assistant engineer. Things went so well, in fact, that Eliza and the children soon joined him. They lived in Rochester and Lockport before David finally purchased a farm near the now-vanished village of Hickory Corners.

Back in Upper Canada, David's elderly father, James, and half-brother, William, had left their families behind, immigrated to Canada in 1843, and moved onto the family farm to keep it going. Eliza returned every six months to take care of paperwork and any other pressing business, and would then go back to her family. The Gibsons had plenty of company in the United States during this time since more than twenty thousand people left Upper Canada over concerns with the Family Compact. Among them was Thomas Alva Edison's father, Samuel Edison of Vienna, Ontario. He too had been charged with treason for his role in the Rebellion and had a £500 reward posted for his capture.

In 1841, the government of Upper Canada instituted many of the changes that the farmers had fought for in 1837, and most of the rebels were pardoned shortly afterwards. By the time David Gibson's pardon came in 1843, the family was so comfortable in New York State that they paid little attention. They even applied for United States citizenship in 1846, but it was a step they would never take. Some years earlier, perhaps feeling the pull of Upper Canada once again, David Gibson did a most unusual thing. He had started to build a house by remote control.

David contracted Toronto brick-maker Henry Neal to produce 133,333 bricks from raw materials found on the

Gibson farm, where a kiln was to be built for the purpose. The project, supervised by John Cummer (the man who took Eliza and the children into his home after the government troops burned the first Gibson house), went off without a hitch. The number of bricks was more than sufficient to build the current Gibson House, which was completed in 1851. As well, there were enough bricks to also build both the shingle mill of Jacob Cummer II (John's brother) just to the north on Yonge Street, and Willowdale School S.S. #4, which stood near the corner of present-day Ellerslie Avenue on the west side of Yonge. David also contracted local tradesmen John Martin for all carpentry and joinery and James Morrison for the masonry work.

The Gibsons returned to Upper Canada in 1848, after David lost his job following an election south of the border that saw the new government cleaning house of former appointees. It was a fairly complicated move, involving many loads of furniture, tools, and personal effects. Once back home, the family set about completing their new house, which, despite the pre-production, was still little more than a finely finished shell. Interestingly, the house would find itself in the same condition over one hundred years later, but that is a later story.

Though it has not been possible to find any mention of where the family stayed while their new home was being completed, it was likely in one of the other houses already standing on the property, built by previous owners, the Willsons, or constructed to house hired hands. David's diaries of the time make mention of repairing fences, cleaning out the well, putting in stoves, and repairing the pump. The Gibsons moved into their beautiful new Georgian-style house in November of 1851. They would keep their farm in New York State, however, and visit it on a regular basis for the remainder of their lives.

Once resettled, David wasted little time getting back to his overachieving ways. In 1851, he was appointed to the First Board of Examiners of the Provincial Land Surveyors —

now the examiner instead of the examinee. In 1853, he was appointed Crown Land commissioner, inspector of Crown Land Agencies, and superintendent of Colonization Roads. It seems that he was missed when he was gone.

His sons James and William, now aged twenty-two and twenty, respectively, had joined him in his surveying business. Youngest son, Peter Silas Gibson, survived his time in the snowbank to graduate from the University of Michigan with an engineering degree in 1864. David built an office addition at the back of the farmhouse and seamlessly continued to survey and farm. The Agricultural Census of 1851 shows two-thirds of the farm being cultivated, with the remaining acres, likely the ones on the west end by the river valley, as "wild." The commodities produced at the farm included wheat, oats, potatoes, wool, pork, beef, and butter.

In 1855, David Gibson petitioned the government for a local post office and suggested the name "Willow Dale," because of the number of willow trees on the property. His request was granted and the post office opened on March 28, 1855, in the Cummers' store on Yonge Street, just north of the Gibson farm. Jacob Cummer II was named the first postmaster, a position he held until 1880, when his brother Samuel took over.

As a little-known aside to David's land holdings, it should be mentioned that in 1854 he was granted 10,000 acres in the District of Parry Sound in appreciation for his contribution to opening up the area for settlement. The land was mostly covered in pine, and David's eldest sons, James and William, came up with the idea of building a sawmill to take advantage of the family's new holdings. The mill wasn't operational until the summer of 1857, but, when the big saw did begin to turn, it became the first business in the area. The pioneer settlement that grew to house and supply the mill workers marked the beginnings of the town of Parry Sound.

Photo by J.V. Salmon, Toronto Public Library, S-4064-B.

Harold Gibson's house is shown here in 1957, the year it was torn down for construction of the Gladys Allison Building of the North York Public Library. The house stood on the southwest corner of Yonge Street and Park Home Avenue.

The Gibson brothers were so busy that they had to hire their Willow Dale neighbours Joseph and Michael Shepard to help them run the mill. Things went well until the outbreak of the American Civil War in April 1861, when the demand for the Gibson's lumber slowed during an economic downturn in the United States, where many of their largest customers were located. Despite David's objections, his sons insisted on selling the land. Its value then proceeded to rise ten-fold over the next several years. Today, its value would be inestimable. After the sale, William worked for his father as a chain-bearer and James worked for his father as a chain-bearer and surveyor. Neither were included in David's will and most sources indicate that the brothers were left so well off after the sale of the sawmill that their father had no need to worry about their futures.

David Gibson died in 1864 at the Russell Hotel in Quebec City on Monday, January 25, after contracting a lung infection on a train trip to one of the meetings he regularly attended in the area. Though he didn't live long enough to celebrate his sixtieth birthday, he accomplished enough to fill several lifetimes. His contributions to Upper Canada and Lower Canada had been phenomenal.

After David's death, the family remained at the Gibson house. David left the farm to his unmarried daughter, Margaret (son William also remained unmarried). Eliza died there in 1887. Before Margaret died in 1868, she sold the farm to her brother, Peter Silas Gibson, who was demonstrating serious need for larger premises. He and his wife, the former Eliza Holmes, would eventually have nine children and twenty-six grandchildren. George Gibson wed Augusta Holmes, the sister of Peter Silas Gibson's wife, Eliza Jane Holmes. They had two sons and six daughters. George died in 1935. Elizabeth Mary Gibson married Walter Armour, whose family farmed near Bathurst and Wilson. They had one daughter, named Lula Ada.

In addition to the Gibson house that stands today, Peter and Eliza's eldest son, Harold, built a house immediately to the south, which was later used as the North York Public Library. It was torn down in 1957 for construction of the Gladys Allison Building of the North York Public Library, which in turn was demolished in 1986 for construction of the current library.

Peter and his older brother James carried on their father's surveying business. James would later move to Oshawa where he opened a book and stationery shop. Peter would serve for thirty-five years as chief engineer of York County, in addition to continuing the family's surveying business, until he suffered a stroke in 1908 and was forced to resign for health reasons. He tendered his resignation to York Township Reeve, George S. Henry, and moved out of the Gibson House and into the house his son Harold had constructed some years earlier.

Peter Silas Gibson died in 1916. His funeral was conducted by the Reverend Thomas Webster Pickett, George S. Henry's father-in-law. Peter's sons, Harold, Wilbert, and Morton carried on with the family's surveying business, now located at the corner of Yonge and Avondale.

After Peter moved to his son's house in 1908, the Gibson farm was rented to the Grainger family, tenant farmers who were also relatives of the Gibsons. They lived in the house and worked the farm for a number of years. When the Graingers retired from farming in 1913, the Gibsons sold the farm, except for the main house and the one acre immediately surrounding it. The house was then rented to a family named Thompson, who lived there until 1938. The remaining acreage was divided among a number of different owners who continued to use it for agricultural purposes.

In 1938, Noel H. Knowles, whose parents clearly had a warped sense of humour when it came to naming children, bought the main house. The farmland was gradually reassembled into one parcel by a company called Parkhome

Photo by J. V. Salmon, Toronto Public Library, S 1-4167.

The Gibson farmhouse is at its nadir, rented out to uncaring tenants in 1957, and deteriorating a little more each day.

Developments, with the intention of building a subdivision. When Noel Knowles died in the mid-1950s, the development company bought the Gibson house and rented it out to tenants who couldn't have cared less about either the farm's history or the house's upkeep. Meanwhile, to the east, north, and south, the subdivisions were closing in around the former Gibson farm.

Noel had spent a considerable sum of money repairing the house but, after a few years at the hands of Parkhome's questionable tenants, the house was once again in a state of disrepair. This is not an unusual ploy for developers to use when they are saddled with an old house they'd rather just tear down. They either rent it out to undesirables to wring the last dollar from the place or they just stand back and let the elements have at it.

The practice, called "demolition by neglect," happens all the time. When the developers know that there are people in the community who would like to see a heritage property preserved, they stop all maintenance on the property in hopes that a roof will cave in or pipes will burst or vandals will damage the structure to the point where the developer can say, "Well, I'm sorry. I'd *like* to save the place but as you can see, it's beyond repair." Unexplained fires also claim more than their fair share of structures caught in limbo between developers and preservationists. In cases like these, the stealth demolition is referred to as "heritage lightning." By the early 1960s, the Gibson farmhouse was in real danger of succumbing to one of these fates. Demolition was being discussed as a real possibility. Then the cavalry rode in.

In this case, the cavalry was the North York Historical Society. Formed in 1960 to document and salvage what they could of the township's heritage, the society celebrated one of their earliest and biggest victories when they were able to convince North York Council to compel Parkhome Developments to sell the house and surrounding property to the Township for the nominal sum of $1.00. When members of the society and council stepped inside for the first time to see what their dollar had bought them, they suddenly realized that the restoration would be no easy task. The house was a mess. A lot of work would have to be done before it was even safe.

By 1965, the historical society had convinced the township to allocate funds for a full restoration of the house as a centennial project to celebrate Canada's one hundredth birthday in 1967. Noted restoration architect Napier Simpson Jr. was commissioned to oversee the project. A better person could not have been chosen, for although Simpson was a stickler for authenticity, he made sure that all structural and practical concerns were also addressed. By 1967, the restoration was completed at a cost of $45,000, a considerable sum at the time and, though the restoration was impeccable, there was still much to be done.

After having visited the house, Miriam Chinsky wrote these evocative words for the *Willowdale Enterprise* newspaper of September 25, 1968.

> The house stands now, a lovely shell, its front door and wide shutters gleaming with ebony paint, its exterior woodwork a spanking white, its ruddy bricks carefully in place, every pane of glass whole-in a tangle of dandelions. Inside, the floorboards are intact, the panelling is perfect, every one of its many fireplaces is ready to function, — and its rooms are dismayingly bare! A few senior citizens have been using it briefly for a toy repairing project, but the dismembered dolls lying about only emphasize the terrible, almost macabre loneliness about the place.

The desolation wouldn't last long.

Soon, a team of dedicated volunteers from the North York Historical Society would transform the house from "a lovely shell" to a fine representation of what the home was like when David Gibson and his family lived there. The family was whole-heartedly behind the project and donated many priceless and poignant heirlooms to furnish the house once again. Included were many of David's books and surveying instruments, as well as a magnificent walnut sideboard for the dining room that David and Elizabeth purchased after they returned from exile in 1848. More everyday items such as dinnerware, candlesticks, and children's dolls were also donated by the family, but perhaps the most moving item of all can be found in the dining room. Remember the workings of the grandfather clock that Elizabeth ran back to salvage after the government troops set fire to the Gibsons' first house? Well, the clock lived to chime again. It seems that, while the family was living in Lockport, they had a local cabinet maker build them a replacement cabinet, and this is the very clock that now stands in the dining room of the Gibson House. Talk about living history....

The house is not the only tell-tale left behind by this remarkable family, however. It is quite likely that if you live in southwestern Ontario, your property was surveyed by the Gibsons at one time or another. Anyone searching old land records will see the Gibson name appearing everywhere, sometimes to the exclusion of all others. Even today, there is a listing for "W.S. Gibson and Sons" in the Toronto *Yellow Pages* under the heading of Surveyors — David's descendants, still showing us the way.

Chapter Fourteen

Samuel Kennedy's Farm

It is always hard to decide whose name to attach to a certain farm when the land may have had dozens of owners over the years, all of whom could lay claim to being the farmer of record. To this point, the most famous names or the earliest names or the most poignant stories related to a particular lot have been chosen. Here, plain old selfishness prevailed and Samuel Kennedy's name was selected. Although not related, the opportunity to see "S. Kennedy" written on the maps of the farms of North York was irresistible.

Samuel Kennedy farmed three separate lots at the corner of Finch and Leslie, but most of his story takes place on the farm that stood on the eastern eighty-two acres of Lot 21-2E. He purchased this lot on the northwest corner of Finch and Leslie from William Johnston in 1883. The farmhouse in the picture had been built by the Johnstons some time earlier, likely in the mid-1850s, when a string of perfect weather resulted in several years of exceptional harvests and many local farmers used the profits to build new brick houses to replace earlier log cabins or frame houses. This farmhouse does in fact bear a striking stylistic resemblance to the house at Spruce Grove Farm a couple of miles to the southeast, which was completed in 1855.

The lot itself had already been home to a number of prominent farmers by the time Samuel took over. The Cummers owned the west half of the lot from 1819 to 1843. Hunters, Harrisons, and Johnstons had all owned portions of the lot before 1883. Afterwards, several smaller lots were carved out of the centre of the lot for houses along Finch Avenue, including one for Robert Risebrough II in 1891.

The first farmland that Samuel purchased in the area lay on the southeast corner of present-day Finch and Leslie. This was the western half of Lot 20-3E that he bought in 1874 from Scottish farmer and former York Township councillor John Henry. The land had previously been cleared and farmed by the Johnston family from 1817 until 1874 when they sold to John Henry. One wonders about John's intentions, or the accuracy of the record-keeping, since the farm was sold to Samuel the same year that John bought it. The Scrace family, English settlers who had arrived in North York in 1831, had been farming the east half of this lot, which ran from Leslie Street over to the Don Valley Parkway, since 1839.

When Samuel bought this land, it was already home to the Zion Schoolhouse, which had been built there on land

Photo by Lorna Gardner, North York Historical Society. NYHS 1100.

This absolutely beautiful brick house captivated visitors for nearly 120 years, from the Johnstons, to Samuel Kennedy, to Joseph Kilgour, to R.Y. Eaton, and the Eglinton Hunt Club. It is shown here in 1967, one year before it was demolished.

donated by William Johnston in 1869. In 1878, Samuel gave some of this farm for the construction of a Temperance Hall, up the hill to the east of the school. It soon became a focal point for community life, hosting church socials, meetings, concerts, and debates. A blacksmith's shop also sat on this lot, on the southeast corner of Leslie and Finch.

Samuel's final purchase involved the northwest fifty acres of Lot 21-3E, on the northeast corner of Finch and Leslie. The eastern half of this lot was still equally divided between the Risebrough and Scrace families, with the Zion Primitive Methodist Church standing on the Scrace property. The southwest corner of this lot, directly south of Samuel, had been farmed by the Harris family since Richard Harris arrived from England in 1839. They would remain on this land into the twentieth century.

By the turn of the century, Samuel Kennedy had assembled a most impressive 235 acres at the corner of Finch and Leslie, some of the prettiest and most productive farmland in the whole area. So what became of all this lovely farmland? Surprisingly, it would remain productive until the mid-1960s.

Photo by Lorna Gardner, North York Historical Society, NYHS 1150.

Joseph Kilgour's beautiful barn, later home to the Eglinton Hunt Club, is shown here being demolished in May 1967, already surrounded by the houses that claimed its former farmland. The faded hunt club logo is still visible.

Sometime around 1910, Joseph Kilgour, who owned Sunnybrook Farm near Bayview and Eglinton, bought Samuel's eighty-seven-acre parcel on the northwest corner of the intersection, including the ten-room main house. Joseph also bought Samuel's ninety-eight-acre lot on the southeast corner, where the Zion School was still operating. Joseph refigured the properties as the centre of his cattle operations and built the beautiful, gambrel-roofed barn, shown in the photographs, to shelter his herds of beef and dairy cattle. He also added an orchard to the farm.

When Joseph died in 1925, his widow Alice donated the majority of their Sunnybrook Farm to the City of Toronto. The land remains today as the spectacular Sunnybrook Park, where the Kilgour stables are still home to horses and a riding school. The former Samuel Kennedy lands were sold to James W. Young in 1926. He held onto the property for a relatively short period of time before selling to R.Y. Eaton in November 1929, just after the stock-market crash. Clearly, the Eatons still had money. A report of the sale in the *Toronto Telegram* of November 23, 1929, mentions that "the southeast corner has been fully cleared and on one point of it a magnificent view of surrounding country is obtainable." This lookout would have been near the current intersection of Don Mills Road and Finch Avenue. R.Y. Eaton converted the Kilgour barn to accommodate horses so his children could be taught to ride. He believed that if you knew how to manage a horse, you would know how to manage people.

R.Y. was not viewed as one of the Toronto Eatons, who were regarded as virtual royalty by the people of Toronto in the early part of the twentieth century. Rather, he was an Irish relation, a nephew of company founder Timothy Eaton,[1] and was regarded as an outsider and treated as such by the family. When Timothy visited his birthplace in Ireland in 1897, Robert Young Eaton was a twenty-one-year-old schoolteacher living on his father's farm. At Timothy's urging, the young R.Y. left teaching to work as a shipping clerk at the Eaton offices in London, England, studying in the evenings and ultimately graduating from the University of London. He was transferred to Eatons' Paris office in 1899, and to Toronto in 1902. He was promoted to secretary in 1904, and to director and first vice-president in 1907, the same year that Timothy's son, John Craig Eaton, took over as president.

When company president Sir John Craig Eaton (he had been knighted by King George V for his efforts in the First World War) died prematurely in 1922, the board appointed R.Y. to head the company, over the objections of Sir John's widow, Lady Eaton. Nevertheless, R.Y. proved to be a good leader, although one universally regarded as cold and aloof. When he took over in 1922, Eatons had a combined total of twenty-three stores, factories, and purchasing offices. When he retired in 1942, that figure had jumped, nearly ten-fold, to a total of 210 separate facilities. In addition to the North York farm, R.Y. had a ten-room, fifteen-acre summer place on Lake Ontario near Port Credit (which he replaced with a new summer home on Georgian Bay when Port Credit was deemed too unfashionable), and a 20,000-square-foot mansion on four acres at One Highland Avenue in Rosedale, which is still standing, though now divided into three separate residences. The Rosedale home could, and did, accommodate six hundred guests at a time.

In the mid-1950s, the Eaton farm was sold to the Eglinton Hunt Club. The club, which had been formed at the Golden Lion Hotel in 1843 as part of the Toronto Hunt Club, had been forced to abandon its spectacular, purpose-built facilities at the corner of Avenue Road and Eglinton by the relentless growth of the city around it. Part of the original clubhouse remains there today as the centre-piece of a town-house development.

The club would remain at the corner of Finch and Leslie until the 1960s, when it was once again uprooted by the encroaching city. The land was sold for development. Joseph Kilgour's barn was torn down in May 1967 and the house that the Johnstons had built over one hundred years earlier was torn down in 1968. Today, the northwest corner of Finch and Leslie is home to a rather unimpressive little nest of assisted housing. To the west, across the railway tracks, are several streets of typical mid-sixties detached and semi-detached houses. To the west of that is the only portion of Samuel Kennedy's farm that still bears a remote resemblance to what it once was. Protected from development by the Metro Toronto and Region Conservation Authority, following the flooding brought on by Hurricane Hazel in 1954, this part of the East Don River Valley that passes through the former farmland is now known as Finch East Park and is well worth a visit.

Photo by Ted Chirnside, Toronto Public Library, TC 355.

This March 31, 1961, photo shows a newly denuded and widened Finch Avenue East, looking east from Page Avenue to the Eglinton Hunt Club barn (originally Joseph Kilgour's splendid barn) on Leslie Street in the left background. The small subdivision, built on former Donald Springer land in 1960, is visible on the southwest corner of Finch and Leslie.

The farmland on the southeast corner of Finch and Leslie was also paved over in the late 1960s. Now it's covered by town-houses, detached houses, and the High Point Condominiums (up where that "magnificent view" was once "obtainable" at the corner of Finch and Don Mills Road). Thankfully, the little one-room Zion School still stands to remind us of what has been lost. Today, it is used as a teaching facility, and for the hosting of classes, plays, and other presentations that depict pioneer life.

The final corner of Samuel Kennedy's farmland met the same fate, but went down swinging. The northeast corner of Finch and Leslie echoed with the sounds of cows, sheep, and chickens until the summer of 1965, when those sounds were replaced by the sounds of earth movers, road graders, hammers, and saws as the last tenant farmers on the former Richard Harris farm were finally evicted and the redevelop-ment began. Samuel's former farm, bordered today by the hydro lines just to the north of the Harris farm, was ploughed under at the same time. Unless one counts the dead-end Fox Hound Court, near the northwest corner of Finch and Leslie, not even a street name exists to remind us of anything that happened here.

CHAPTER FIFTEEN

The Johnston Family Farms

IT HAS ALREADY BEEN NOTED HOW SOME PIONEER FAMILIES, SUCH as the Risebroughs, have made the work of genealogists and historians more difficult by giving their sons the same first names as their fathers and grandfathers. With the Johnstons, this phenomenon has not only been duplicated, but carried to the next level by the frequent elimination of the letter "t" from the family's surname in official records. It's not the family's fault of course and an honest mistake since the two spellings *sound* virtually identical. Thankfully, the Johnsons — sorry, Johns*t*ons — have made things a little easier by doing their farming in a well-defined area around Leslie and Finch, so even if a couple of the exact names are unclear, the family narrative is not that difficult to follow.

Some sources list a Thomas Johnston as the first member of the family to arrive from Sligo, Ireland, in the early 1800s. This may well have been true, but the first Johnston to appear on deeds in the area was James Johnston, who was granted Lot 22-3E by the Crown in 1816, and who bought the west half of Lot 20-3E, on the southeast corner of Leslie and Finch, as well as the eastern quarter of Lot 22-2E, in 1817. Other sources describe Thomas arriving in North York in 1837. The land records clearly give the nod to James. It is equally clear that the

Johnstons would continue to accumulate farmland in the area for nearly eighty years after James's first land grant, and would continue to farm in North York for nearly 140 years — an incredible demonstration of perseverance, matched only by two or three other families in the entire area.

The pattern of the Johnstons' land acquisitions was somewhat unusual in that they never really purchased entire lots. In fact, James Johnston's original Crown grant to Lot 22-3E was the only time that the family would ever acquire an entire two-hundred-acre lot in one fell swoop. They would eventually own over six hundred acres in the area, but it was all acquired in increments of fifty or one hundred acres at a time. As noted, James himself had assembled 350 acres by 1817.

Twenty more years would pass before Thomas's name appeared on a deed when he bought the southern half of lot 24-3E, three-quarters-of-a-mile south of Steeles Avenue, between Leslie Street and Woodbine Avenue. This was the most northerly land that the family would ever farm. James passed away and willed his farmland to his wife, Lois, and their six sons in 1837, with the provision that the sons pay an annual stipend to their sisters who, inherited household goods and furnishings but not farmland.

Photographer unknown, North York Historical Society, NYHS 1229.

Thomas Johnston's house on Lot 23-3E, shown here in the 1890s in its original configuration, was located on the east side of Leslie Street between Finch and Steeles Avenues.

For the next sixty years, the family would continue to buy more land and expand their farms. They would also get into milling when John Johnston bought the Reading Mills, in the middle of Lot 22-2E, from John Cummer in 1868. By all accounts, the Johnstons took a progressive approach to the business of farming, as was the case when Thomas was cred-ited with owning the first threshing machine in York County. The family was also involved in many community activities and hosted the first meetings of the local Primitive Methodist Church in James's house.

For nearly a century and a half, the Johnstons' names fluttered down through North York history like autumn

Photo by Ted Chirnside, Toronto Public Library, TC-365.

The last ride, looking east along Finch Avenue East, from Page Avenue to Leslie Street, in March of 1961. A group of riders set out from the Edwin Ness stables, heading north across Finch to the still-open land in that direction. At one point, the Johnstons' farms covered virtually all of the land in this photo.

leaves. Here is a roughly chronological list of some of the names as they appeared on the deeds to the farms from 1817 to 1955: James, John, Thomas, Thomas Jr., Henry, Ellen, another John, another James, William, another Henry, Silas, Lucy, Robert J., Silas W., William H., Fanny, and, finally, Robert Wesley Johnston. The last two names on the list, Fanny and Robert Wesley, son of Robert James Johnston, may be the most interesting to current residents of North York, since they appear to be among the last to farm Johnston family lands.

In 1934, Fanny sold the east half of Lot 20-2E, on the southwest corner of Leslie and Finch. The farm had been in the family since 1868 and stretched from Leslie Street westwards towards the present-day Page Avenue. It was a particularly beautiful farm, even by North York standards, embracing as it did the majestic sweep of the East Don Valley. The farm's new owner in 1934 was one Joseph Thadeus Sutherland Cannon, a Toronto stockbroker who seemed to be weathering the Depression rather well. He bought the Johnston farm to use as a country estate. The farm already featured two houses and a large barn, to which he added a beautiful new stone house that stands to this day at 10 Woodthrush Court. He christened his new estate "Bridleridge."

In 1940, the western fifty acres of Bridleridge, including the main house, were sold to Charles T. McMullen for somewhere in the neighbourhood of $35,000. Imagine going back in time and making *that* purchase? The McMullens were avid equestrians and enjoyed riding their horses through the valley lands until they sold the property in 1950. This time the new owner, Edwin Ness, had a commercial venture in mind. Edwin converted the property to accommodate a riding school and stable, but mother nature and urban sprawl had a couple of surprises up their sleeves that would soon still the sound of hoofbeats.

Shortly before midnight, on October 15, 1954, Hurricane Hazel roared through Toronto with life-altering results. Eighty-one people were killed, including five volunteer firemen whose truck was swept into the raging Humber River. Houses and businesses in the river valleys were severely damaged or swept away altogether. In the aftermath of the tragedy, the City of Toronto created the Metropolitan Toronto and Region Conservation Authority to oversee the valley lands of the Humber, Rouge, and Don Rivers and their tributaries. Further development in the river valleys was forbidden and private land in the valleys was expropriated to allow for the implementation of flood control measures.

At the same time all of this was happening, the new subdivision of Bayview Village was being constructed directly to the southwest of Edwin Ness's riding stables. It was a perfect storm of change, and yet the stables held on for a surprisingly long time, isolated as they were on Bayview Village's northern border. The group of people on horseback setting out at the corner of Finch and Page Avenues in 1961 likely participated in one of the last rides, since the surrounding area to the southwest was now fully built out.

Soon the riding stables were gone, and, by 1962, the last houses in Bayview Village were built in the area surrounding Heathview and Page Avenues, looking distinctly different than their 1950s neighbours to the south. The river valley was now in the hands of the municipal government. This latter change preserved a spectacular piece of the Johnstons' original farmland. Now known as the East Don Parkland, the trail through the river valley offers the twenty-first-century visitor a tantalizing chance to escape the hustle and bustle of the surrounding tableland. This farm will be revisited in the somewhat bizarre tale of oilman Donald Springer and the massive barn that he converted into a house on former Johnston farmland in the 1940s.

In 1955, Robert Wesley Johnston sold the farm his family had farmed for four generations and retired to a house in Willowdale. The farm on the southeast corner of today's Leslie Street and McNicoll Avenue had been started by Robert's great-grandfather, Thomas, in 1853. That was the year that Thomas, who had emigrated from Ireland some years earlier, was granted the northwest fifty acres of the lot — Lot 23-3E. Eleven years later the family would add another fifty acres to the farm when they purchased the southwest corner of the lot. The Johnstons now owned the western half of the lot, while the James Bell family of Spruce Lane Farm owned the eastern half.

The Johnston farm was handed down through the years as each new generation took the reins. Thomas Johnston Junior took over from his father, who died in 1869, two years after confederation. Following Thomas Junior was *his* son, Robert James Johnston, who helped build the Zion schoolhouse on Johnston family farmland in 1869. In 1902, Robert Wesley Johnston was born on the family farm. As he grew up, the Zion School would loom large in his life. He attended the school as a boy and later served as a school trustee. He even met his wife there, the former Agnes Euphemia McDougall, who taught at the school. They would work together on the farm, raising three daughters — Mary, Roberta, and Audrey — along the way, surrounded by countless relatives on the neighbouring Johnston farms. Robert Johnston's farm included pigs, chickens, a dairy herd, and acres of grain. The family turned part of their front yard into a vegetable patch to supply their own larder and also grew raspberries, strawberries, apples, and pears. Robert travelled into the city on a regular basis, selling hay to Toronto delivery companies who depended on horse-drawn wagons to deliver milk, bread, ice, and many other commodities well into the 1950s.

Photographer unknown, North York Historical Society, NYHS 1242.

Robert Wesley Johnston, the last Johnston to farm in North York, is pictured here circa 1910 as a determined looking young lad with his sister, Zelma May (Mrs. John Johnston), and their parents, Mr. and Mrs. Robert James Johnston.

By the 1950s, property taxes in North York were spiralling out of control as the demand for postwar housing reached a fever pitch. When 1955 rolled around, Robert, though not an old man, was old enough to read the writing

Photo by Dorothy Milne, North York Historical Society, NYHS 861.

Thomas Johnston's house is shown in 1964 after subsequent additions and renovations.

on the wall. When he started farming in the 1920s, the population of the newly created Township of North York was somewhere in the region of 7,000 people. By 1955, that figure had exceeded 150,000 and was increasing rapidly. By 1963 there would be over 300,000 people in North York. These people all needed somewhere to live and Robert decided that his farm would be as good a place as any, so, in 1955, he sold it to developers who were planning a subdivision that they called Hillcrest Village.

Photos from 1964 show the family home still standing in a livable condition, but by year's end it was gone. It wouldn't be until the late 1960s that the new subdivision was completed, however. This was not an unusual situation as much of the farmland in North York was bought on speculation, before any rezoning, financing, blueprints, or permits had been finalized. In addition, North York would have had to agree to the construction of new roads, sewers, and other essential infrastructure. These steps often took years. In the interim, developers would rent the land to any farmers still working in the area and then use the farmhouses as sales offices for the new subdivisions. The houses were usually the last physical traces of the farms that once surrounded them. When the subdivisions were sold out, the farmhouses, no longer needed as sales offices, would be demolished. Other Johnston farmhouses in the area also survived into the 1960s, but not beyond.

Robert Wesley Johnston died at Branson Hospital on December 20, 1966, survived by his wife, daughters, sister, and three grandchildren. He had not yet reached official retirement age, but he had enjoyed his own eleven-year retirement that was spent gardening, restoring antique furniture, and involving himself with the Willowdale United Church. His pallbearers included fellow North York farmers Robert McDougall, Worts Gooderham, and Alfred Trimble, as well as newly retired district police chief and former farmer, John Harrison.

What remarkable thread ran through this family that would see farms passed seamlessly down through the generations for nearly 150 years? What would they think of their farms now? What would they think of *us*?

Chapter Sixteen

The Somewhat Bizarre Tale of Donald Springer

Donald Matheson Springer died in Charlottesville, Virginia, on February 19, 1952. The barn that Donald converted to a house in 1947 stood on Allview Crescent, near the corner of Leslie and Finch, until it was demolished on May 6, 2003, roughly 120 years after it had been built.

Donald Springer was born in Lisbon, Ohio, on June 13, 1898. He lived a solitary, successful life, much of it in Canada, and left us this remarkable structure, which in the end proved unworthy of our respect — unfortunately far too typical, though still sad. Imagine how much more welcoming and attractive North York would be today if even a fraction of our destructive tendencies had been redirected to preservation?

Donald Springer interrupted his studies at the University of Michigan to serve in the United States Navy during the First World War. Following the war, he completed his studies, graduating with a bachelor of science in chemical engineering in 1919. He put his degree to immediate use when he joined the Standard Oil Company of New York and was posted overseas as a manager in Ceylon (now Sri Lanka) and India. He remained there for a remarkably long time, not returning to North America until 1930. When he came back, he settled in Toronto where he formed Toronto Fuels Limited. Other companies under his umbrella included Liquid Fuels Limited, Fueloil Sales Limited, Fueloil and Equipment Limited, and General Oil Heating Limited — perfectly tapping into this city's changeover from coal to oil as the preferred method of heating. If he wasn't wealthy when he returned from India, he certainly would be before long.

Though Donald never married, he was an active member of local society. He belonged to the Ontario Jockey Club, the Rosedale Golf and Country Club, the Toronto Hunt Club, the Eglinton Hunt Club, the University Club, the American Mens' Club, the Advertising and Sales Club, and the Granite Club, where he lived for a time at 63 St. Clair Avenue West. In addition, he belonged to the Board of Trade and was a member of the Opera Festival Board. In Virginia, he belonged to the Farmington Country Club. He was always interested in helping young people get ahead and established a number of scholarships at the University of Toronto and his *alma mater*, the University of Michigan, while an officer of the Advertising and Sales Club.

Photo by Lorna Gardner, North York Historical Society, NYHS 1169.

The beautiful home that Donald Springer created from an existing barn on his property in 1947 is shown here as it appeared in 1967. It would stand until being demolished on May 6, 2003.

Shortly after the end of the Second World War, Donald Springer bought a beautiful corner of one of the former Johnston farms on the southwest corner of Leslie and Finch, part of Lot 20-2E. The property included the right-of-way for the Canadian National Railway line, the tableland between Leslie Street and the East Don Valley, and part of the valley lands as well. When Donald took possession, a house, stables, garage, and large barn were already standing on the property. It would be his conversion of the Johnson family barn into a magnificent home and the longevity of the house that would alert people to his existence many years later.

Donald's new property proved a boon to his fellow hunt-club members who were being hounded by the burgeoning city to find new places to pursue the inedible, since development was rapidly claiming their old haunts. They were welcomed at Donald's, however, and must have enjoyed the area, since several years later the Eglinton Hunt Club bought the former Samuel Kennedy farm, directly to the north, from R.Y. Eaton, to serve as their new headquarters.

Donald was also a charter member of the first North York Planning Board, which was established on September 25, 1946, to oversee the development of North York. He, like his fellow board member Earl Bales, would also serve as chairman of the board. While in that role in 1950 and 1951, he ruled that septic tanks would not be permitted in any new subdivisions, a very drastic change to what was then common practice, and one of many signs that North York's days as a farming community were coming to an end.

When Donald died in 1952, he left an estate in the neighbourhood of $600,000. He had no heirs or survivors, other than his mother in Ohio, so his will directed that his estate be divided among a number of his favourite causes. The University of Toronto and the University of Western Ontario were beneficiaries of his generosity, but the bulk of his fortune went to funds he had set up to see to the care and education of needy children and to provide financial assistance to young adults who would otherwise not be able to attend college or university.

After his death, the little farm was bought by a Reginald Hall. The farmland was subdivided in 1960, and a subdivision centred on Alamosa Drive and Appian Drive was constructed. Mr. Hall continued to live in the converted barn until 1973, when it was sold to another family. The house continued to be inhabited until 2001 when the children, who inherited it, put it up for sale, hoping someone would want to restore it.

After a year passed and no one wanted the barn as a home, it was sold to Bayfin Homes. The developer bought it in February of 2003 and demolished it on May 6 of the same year. Jonathan Winberg, project coordinator for Bayfin, went the extra mile when he donated some of the 120-year-old timbers to Black Creek Pioneer Village. Two new rather ordinary-looking homes were then built on the site of Donald Springer's converted barn. It seems unlikely that anyone will be writing their story in the twenty-second century.

CHAPTER SEVENTEEN

From the Macaulays to James Dean

THIS FARMLAND HAD IT ALL — A JUDGE, A MANSION, AN INN-keeper, a doctor, a reverend, a reverend-doctor, a succession of farmers, and even its own James Dean. Today, it is pleasant, leafy, and residential. Lot 25-2E was always beautiful, bordered on its western edge by the same stretch of the East Don River that runs through Mazo de la Roche's Windrush Hill and on its eastern border by the German Mills Creek. It stretched along the south side of Steeles Avenue from Bayview Avenue to Leslie Street. Like most of this part of North York, it was beautiful, rolling land with deep river valleys and fresh forested vistas around every turn. Farmhouses and farmland survived here until 1972. Today, although all that is left are stories and photographs, it is still quite possible to conjure up a feeling of what must have been.

It was most unusual for the Crown to grant farm lots to women in the eighteenth century, but there weren't many women like Elizabeth Macaulay. A childhood friend of Elizabeth Simcoe — the wife of Upper Canada's first lieutenant governor, John Graves Simcoe — the former Elizabeth Hayter had married Dr. James Macaulay in 1790, after he had served as a surgeon in Simcoe's regiment during the American Revolutionary War. In 1791, the two families travelled together from Britain to Upper Canada and settled in Newark, today's Niagara-on-the-Lake. In 1792, the lieutenant governor decided to move the capital of Upper Canada to York.

The Macaulays accompanied the Simcoes once again, and, when they arrived in York, Dr. Macaulay was charged with creating the new town's first hospital and medical board. He also asked for, and was granted, an astonishing amount of Crown land, including 1,600 acres for himself, 1,200 acres for Elizabeth, and 660 acres for each of the couple's children. Part of the land granted to Elizabeth was the two-hundred-acre Lot 25-2E on Steeles Avenue.

The family's first home, named Teraulay Cottage after a combination of James's and Elizabeth's family names, was located in the town of York, on the site where the Holy Trinity Church would later be constructed. Other family members also built homes nearby, and soon the area running from Yonge Street to Osgoode Hall was known as Macaulaytown — the first suburb in Toronto. James and Elizabeth witnessed the dawn of a whole new society, yet they could never have imagined what the little cluster of log cabins that was once the town of York has exploded into today. Macaulaytown is now covered by the Eaton Centre, Old City Hall, New City Hall, office buildings, and hotels. After Elizabeth died in 1809, James would marry Rachel Crookshank, another Loyalist and close friend of Elizabeth Simcoe. Rachel's brother, George Crookshank, is featured in the chapter on Lot 24-1E. Dr. Macaulay retired to York in 1817, after spending twelve years in Quebec overseeing hospital construction and serving as medical examiner. He died in 1822.

The Macaulay children capitalized on the head start that their parents had offered them and built on the family's accomplishments in most impressive ways. Youngest son Allan was the first missionary to be put in charge of St. John's Anglican Church in York Mills. Born in 1804, he was still a young student studying under Dr. John Strachan, then Archdeacon of York, when he was ordained as Reverend Allan Macaulay on October 28, 1827. His primary duty was to establish regular Sunday services at St. John's, the second church to be built in this part of Upper Canada after the initial log St. James' on King Street, which opened in 1807. He was also part of the consecration of the second limestone St. James' on September 2, 1828. Tragically, Allan was plagued by ill health of an unrecorded nature, which, despite his bravest efforts, sometimes prevented him from conducting the Sunday services at St. John's. On those Sundays he would still try to drag himself out of his sick bed to at least attend the services, even if he was too ill to perform them. He died in 1830 at the age of twenty-six.

The Macaulay sons were all educated at Dr. Strachan's schools in Cornwall and York, and although not all of them entered the clergy as Allan did, his brother William would leave a religious legacy in one small Ontario town that resonates to this day.

Shortly after William Macaulay was ordained, he moved to Picton, where he founded the local Anglican congregation and became the community's early spiritual leader. Prince Edward County was a favourite with United Empire Loyalists at the time, and William, as the son of a prominent Loyalist, had been granted much of the land that now comprises the town of Picton when he was just nine years old. Though well-born, he was generous to a fault, donating land for two churches and the courthouse, as well as personally surveying the new streets that were laid out in the town. Actually, he really wasn't much of a businessman, and, though he also worked as a miller and operated a wharf back when Prince Edward County was a major shipping centre, his lack of killer instinct soon landed him in financial difficulty. He was known to sell his land below market value when he was dealing with a deserving farmer who was short of cash. He also allowed tenant farmers on his land to fall far behind in their rent, as he had great faith in his fellow man and believed that, ultimately, all would turn out well. The construction of his own rectory brought him to the edge of bankruptcy and resulted in his older brother, John Simcoe Macaulay, being given his financial power of attorney. William was now free to concentrate on his ministry, knowing that his other affairs were in capable hands.

The rectory, when completed around 1839, was considered the finest house in the county. The red-brick, neo classical-style home was perfectly proportioned and beautifully detailed. Featuring every modern convenience of the day, it was situated next to the newly constructed St. Mary Magdalene Anglican Church. William was also the chaplain to the Legislative Assembly of Upper Canada for a time, but it was his work in Picton, where he lived out the rest of his life while serving as rector from 1827 to 1874, that would define his legacy and leave us with one of the only traces of the Macaulay family to still physically exist. Today, after thousands of volunteered hours, the rectory has been meticulously restored to its mid-nineteenth-century perfection. This breathtakingly beautiful restoration is well worth a visit. The Anglican church, now a museum, is just next door.

John Simcoe Macaulay, the eldest brother, who took over William's finances, was a colonel in the Queen's Rangers before serving on the Legislative Council of Upper Canada from 1839 to 1841. He was also a magistrate, postmaster, surveyor general, inspector general, and an agent of the Bank of Upper Canada in Kingston. He retired to England in 1843, where he died in 1855 in his sixty-fourth year. The final son, James Macaulay, was arguably the most impressive of all.

James was born in 1793, two years after John and one year before William. He was drawn to the legal profession where he was called to the bar in 1822. He worked extremely hard and was appointed as a judge in 1829, the same year he assumed ownership of Lot 25-2E. He served as chief justice from 1849 to 1856, and was knighted just before he died in 1859. At the time of his death, he had assembled the most impressive title of Chief Justice, the Honourable Sir James Buchanan Macaulay, and yet he was also remembered for his commitment to helping the less fortunate.

Ten years after Sir James's death, his widow sold their home, near the southwest corner of Yonge and College Streets, to the Bishop Strachan School, which remained there for forty-five years until the school moved to its present campus on Lonsdale Road. The Macaulays' former home sat vacant for a while before being demolished for the construction of the T. Eaton Company Limited's College Street store that opened in 1930. Sir James's daughter, Elizabeth, continued the family's involvement with the Anglican Church when she married the "right-irascible" Reverend Doctor Richard Mitchele.

Richard Mitchele was a graduate of Trinity College in Dublin. His first posting in Upper Canada was to Holy Trinity Church, which stood on land that the Macaulays had donated to the church when they vacated their first home in Upper Canada. When he first arrived in York he was simply the Reverend *Mr.* Richard Mitchele. It wouldn't be until 1859, after he received his LL.D. degree from Trinity College in Dublin, that he became the Reverend Doctor Mitchele. He was posted to St. John's after his stint at Holy Trinity, and arrived in York Mills in July of 1852 with a fervent desire to set the records straight — literally.

It seems that certain parts of the original church register had been filled up by 1849, six years after the construction of the current brick church. A new register had been obtained for recording marriages, baptisms, and burials, while vestry minutes continued to be recorded in the old registry. In addition, the church wardens at St. John's had started a new book to keep track of financial records beginning in 1851, though, curiously, previous financial records remain unaccounted for to this day. It comes as no surprise then that the new reverend was less than pleased with his introduction to the new parish, since the church places great importance in proper record-keeping. He did not deliver his verbal report on the state of affairs at St. John's until 1854, and, when he did, it was tinged with his annoyance at the missing records. Nonetheless, it was he who consecrated the church on October 18, 1854.

Dr. Mitchele helped improve the church's finances, but a financial depression in 1857 burdened little settlements like York Mills until early in the 1860s. Before the congregation of St. John's had fully recovered from the depression, Dr. Mitchele left on an extended trip to England in 1861. This was to be the first of several unexplained absences that were born with mild annoyance by the congregation as they welcomed a series of temporary clergy. It was during this first absence that nineteen-year-old John Squire was hired as sexton of St. John's, a position he held until his death in 1931. Dr. Mitchele returned in the summer of 1862, only to disappear again in the summer of 1863.

Courtesy of North York Historical Society, NYHS 319.

This elegant Georgian home graced Lot 25-2E near Bayview and Steeles until 1972. Built by William Dickson over one hundred years earlier, the house was photographed by Lorna Gardner in 1962.

Dr. Mitchele reappeared at St. John's, quite unexpectedly, in August of 1864. In September, he called a vestry meeting where he himself recorded the minutes in a strong, angry hand and used the same violent pen strokes to slash the word "cancelled" across the minutes of all meetings that had been held in his absence. Two months later he returned to England and never came back, while St. John's remains a cornerstone of the community to this day.

The Macaulays' involvement with Lot 25-2E had ended many years earlier when, in 1832, Sir James B. Macaulay sold the south half of the lot to William Dickson, who had lived in North York for over thirty years, and the north half of the lot to Joseph Abraham (also spelled Abrahams in some records), proprietor of the Green Bush Inn at Yonge and Steeles in 1833. Downtown Toronto remembered the Macaulays with a series of streets that were named after the family, including Elizabeth, Terauly, Macaulay, Louisa, Hayter, and James Streets.

William Dickson bought the one hundred acre southern half of Lot 25-2E for slightly less than £150, a relatively small amount for North York farmland at the time, and likely indicative of the fact that the property had probably not been cleared or built upon. This seems reasonable since the Macaulays were quite busy indeed with their pursuits in town. Well-connected Loyalists like the Macaulays were often granted title to their land even if they never lifted a finger to fulfill the conditions that other settlers had to complete before the Crown would hand over the deed. This practice resulted in many uncleared road allowances, further impeding the already difficult travel of the early settlers, and becoming one of many ongoing grievances that would eventually lead to the Upper Canada Rebellion of 1837. But back to William Dickson.

It would be interesting to report that this is the same William Dickson who emigrated from Scotland to Lower Canada in 1785, built the first brick house in Upper Canada after settling in Niagara in 1792, killed William Weekes, a member of the House of Assembly, in a duel in 1806, bought 95,000 acres of former Six Nations land for £15,000, where he built the town of Galt, and served on the Legislative Council of Upper Canada, but that is not the case. It seems that there were several prominent William Dicksons in Upper Canada at the time, and this Dickson was one of the other ones. Fortunately, he also knew how to build a brick house.

The photo of Dickson's home shows evidence of several later additions, including the enclosed vestibule, and wings on either side of the main structure. The six-over-six-pane sash windows are likely a later and much easier to clean version of the twelve-over-twelve pattern common to Georgian houses of the mid-nineteenth century. (As roads became smoother, it became easier to transport larger pieces of glass). William Dickson was by no means a newcomer to North York, having bought Lot 16-1W from the original grantee, James Johnson, in 1798. He sold the lot to Joseph Shepard in 1802, where, thirty-three years later, Joseph would build the house that stands to this day at 90 Burndale Avenue.

Dickson continued to be involved in business as well as farming after moving to North York. In 1856, he bought the Reading Mills that had been built by the Cummer family in the East Don Valley, roughly half-a-mile south of his new house. The mill site included a sawmill that had been built in 1819, and a gristmill and woollen mill that had been completed in 1851. Strangely, the Cummers bought the mills back from William just two years later. He must have kept them running as a profitable business, and was by now probably looking forward to retirement. When Dickson died in 1866, he left the farm on the southern half of Lot 25-2E to his son John Dickson, who remained on the property until 1883, when he sold the farm to a Benjamin Madill.

When Sir James Macaulay sold the north half of this lot to Joseph Abraham in 1833, he would have no idea that this transaction would be used as an excuse to tell the tale of the Green Bush Inn, which stood on the northeast corner of Yonge and Steeles, just outside of Willowdale.

When Joseph Abraham bought the north half of Lot 25-2E in 1833, he had already been operating the original Green Bush Inn on the northeast corner of Yonge and Steeles for three years. The picturesque inn, named after a large balsam fir tree that stood in the front yard, was situated on a sixty-acre parcel of Lot 26-1E that Joseph had purchased from original Crown grantee William L. Willson for £350.

The inn was situated near the present-day gas station on the corner, and served farmers and travellers for over thirty years. The end came sadly after the inn's stables caught fire and eleven horses, belonging to farmers from the north who were staying at the inn, perished. The tragedy took the heart out of Joseph Abraham and tainted the previously solid reputation of his inn. He moved on, taking the wooden sign with the picture of the balsam tree that hung outside of the inn, and re-established a second Green Bush Inn on Lot Street on the outskirts of the town of York, near today's intersection of Yonge and Shuter Streets.

The farm where the Green Bush Inn once stood, survived into the twentieth century before finally being subdivided in 1949. The inn was thought to have reverted to the role of private residence for Samuel Francis and his wife, who lived there from 1894–1904, after vacating the farm in Thornhill they owned until 1929, when they sold it to Charles Heintzman. But there is still one Green Bush Inn yet to be heard from, and though it isn't the original, it was certainly the longest-lived.

While Joseph Abraham was running the Green Bush Inn on the northeast corner of Yonge and Steeles, John Morely built a tavern on the northwest corner of the same intersection in 1847. Purchased ten years later by Thomas Steele, an innkeeper from Yorkshire, England, and whose family name still graces Toronto's northern-most avenue, the new tavern gained fame as Steeles Hotel, then as the Poplar House, and ultimately as yet another Green Bush Inn. Steele ran the inn for thirty years, before dying there in 1877. His wife Milcah then took over, followed by their son John in 1882. The business thrived for a surprisingly long time by adapting to keep up with changing times. In 1906, the inn was being used as hunt-club clubhouse, and, in 1909, John Steele sold the inn to an Ida Spink, who ran it as a tea room.

In 1931, the building's commercial days were brought to a close when Thomas Collins bought the inn and converted it to a private residence. He demolished the large rear wing on the north side of the inn and moved the main front portion of the inn further west along Steeles Avenue to make room for a gas station — or "service station," as they were once known when they actually provided service. The move could probably fill a chapter on its own since it took place with the Collinses still in residence.

The Collins family had emigrated from England before the First World War, although both Thomas and his son returned to fight with the British and Canadian forces. Years later, when the family decided to move the Green Bush Inn further west to serve as their permanent residence, they were told by the man hired to do the job that the move would take six days. It ended up taking six weeks as two over-worked horses and a gang of workmen hoisted the house onto wooden rollers and dragged it inch by inch to its new location. As the building creaked and groaned along Steeles Avenue, the plaster ceilings began to crack and shower the Collinses with that horrible plaster dust that gets into everything. Mrs. Collins took some months to get over the ritual ordeal of cooking for her own family, as well as a gang of hungry workmen, for the month-and-a-half it took to drag the old inn to its new home.

Thomas Collins lived here until 1938. After he died, his spinster daughter Ruth lived in the house until 1962, when she sold the property to Joseph Arrigo and J.V. DiGuillo for commercial development. Ruth, a talented illustrator and author, retired to an apartment in Newtonbrook, where she continued to write and illustrate successful children's books. A student of noted Canadian illustrator C.W. Jefferys at the Ontario College of Art, she contributed illustrations to one of the most valuable research tools on North York — the book *150 Years at St. John's, York Mills* by M. Audrey Graham.

Photographer unknown, Toronto Public Library, SC 568-232-2.

The Green Bush Inn and Tea Garden is neat as a pin and open for business on the northwest corner of Yonge and Steeles in 1920.

After Ruth sold the old place, the new owners condemned it to demolition by neglect. It deteriorated for seven years, until it was sold to William Popovich, who wanted the land to expand his adjacent auto dealership — Yonge-Steeles Motors. While he was wrangling for rezoning and a demolition permit, Popovich leased the house to landscaper George Bankuti who used the main floor as a residence and office while renting the upstairs rooms out for forty dollars a month. The front yard soon filled up with bricks, rolls of sod, mountains of topsoil, and terra-cotta planters, while eight people lived upstairs in squalor.

Ironically, a lifeline was thrown to the old Green Bush Inn, even as William Popovich was preparing its death notice. It seems that students at York University had an awareness of the inn and expressed a desire to move it to their campus at Keele and Steeles and restore it as a campus pub. Noted architect Napier B. Simpson completed a feasibility study, which concluded that the building was well-suited to just such a repurposing. His report contained the following passage: "In view of the historic and architectural value of this particular building the idea was received with great enthusiasm, and particularly because it also indicated that the young people of our nation are becoming aware of and appreciate our heritage."[1] The students began to hold fundraisers to raise the money for the restoration. Then, the North York Board of Control stumbled onto the scene.

The controllers visited the property on May 14, 1969, and were appalled by what they saw, especially Mayor James Service, who was quoted in the following day's *Globe and Mail* when he called the building "Just a decrepit hollow shell."[2] Controller Basil Hall sank to the depths of bureaucracy when he declared in the same article that the building could not be moved into North York because North York no longer allowed the construction of wooden buildings. The York

University student committee charged with getting the ball rolling estimated moving and restoration costs at $133,000, the same amount that a new brick building would have cost. They were only asking North York for $5,000 to help with the moving costs. By July, the students had already secured cash and pledges that topped $30,000. William Popovich offered to donate the building to the students' committee. Then, the hammer dropped.

North York Council met on July 7 and voted to accept the Board of Control's recommendation that the students' request to move the inn be denied. Alderman Murray Chusid provided a voice in the wilderness when he was quoted in *The Toronto Daily Star* of July 8, 1969, as saying; "If they want to drink beer in a historic building, let them."[3] Though William Popovich had agreed to delay demolition until November to allow the students a chance to appeal the borough's decision to the Ontario Municipal Board, salvation was not forthcoming and the poor old inn mouldered for another two and a half years before it was finally demolished in January of 1972.

Local history buffs salvaged what they could, including pine boards from the interior that were up to twenty-four inches wide, from trees of a size that will never be seen here again. Phyllis Bentzen summed up this sad event most eloquently in the February 2nd issue of the *Mirror/Enterprise* when she said: "The loss of Green Bush Inn is mostly a loss of opportunity. Our past is brief, and unless we begin to preserve some tangible evidence it will remain so."[4]

In 1879, Joseph Abraham sold his farm on the north half of Lot 25-2E to John Coates (also spelled 'Coats' in some records). Architectural details, such as the prominent bay window, indicate that the house pictured at 327 Steeles Avenue East was probably built by Coates shortly after he bought the farm. In 1883, John Dickson sold his family's farm on the south half of the lot to Benjamin Madill. The Coates farmed

Photo by Dorothy Milne, North York Historical Society, NYHS 785.

This lovely farmhouse on the south side of Steeles Avenue East, just east of Bayview, was photographed by Dorothy Milne on March 1, 1964. It would remain standing until January 1973.

their new land until 1895 when they sold to Archelaus Willis, who sold to Thomas Ford just one year later. The Madills stayed on their farm until the end of the nineteenth century. Henry Madill was the architect who designed the original Earl Haig Collegiate that opened its doors in the autumn of 1930.

By 1910 the lot had been divided into east/west halves rather than its traditional north/south split. Thomas's son Joseph Ford was living in the former Coates house and running a small farm on a sixteen-acre remnant of his family's farm, on the southeast corner of Bayview and Steeles. The eastern half of Lot 25-2E was now owned by one J. Fisher, while James Dean made his first appearance as the farmer of record on the middle eighty-four acres. Two houses were shown on the Dean lot, including William Dickson's mansion and the more humble farmhouse pictured here at 337 Steeles Avenue East in 1964.

Farmland survived on this lot until the mid-1960s. Estate homes began cropping up in this area in the 1930s, such as Mazo de la Roche's Windrush Hill, just across Bayview from the Ford farm. Benjamin Fish's gristmill was converted to a private residence and studio in 1938 by artist Angus Macdonald on the northeast corner of Bayview and Steeles. Aerial photos from 1947 show that Lot 25-2E was still farmland, except for the pictured houses and their barns and outbuildings, but, by the mid-1960s, the city was knocking at the door.

Developers staked out the western half of the lot first, from west of the CN railway tracks all the way over to Bayview Avenue. By 1969 a small subdivision, including roadways such as Bestview Drive, Laureleaf Road South, and Harrington Crescent, was underway, followed by a small shopping centre at the corner of Steeles and Laureleaf. In typical fashion, the old houses were the last to go, but as the sun rose on 1973, there were no traces of North York's farming heritage left to catch its rays. A high-rise apartment complex called the Gates of Bayview was erected near the lot's western boundary on Old English Lane, and, by the 1980s, the last undeveloped tract on the southwest corner of Leslie and Steeles offered townhouses, detached houses, and the Gibson Retirement Community.

Thanks to the river valleys, however, some interesting parkland still beckons the weary urbanite with a glimpse of the way things used to be. Both Saddletree Park near Leslie and Steeles, and Garnier Park at Bayview and Steeles, lead to the East Don Valley that the intrepid traveller may follow all the way south to Lake Ontario, some twelve miles distant. Bestview Park begins in the middle of the lot, where the Dickson house once stood, and runs south for a quarter-of-a-mile to the other side of the German Mills Creek, where Dr. Herbert Bruce's farm once stood on Lot 24-2E, after he moved north from his Annandale farm at Bayview and Lawrence. This park offers a tantalizing glimpse of how beautiful this land must have been when there were still farms in North York.

It is saddening to look at the photos of these farmhouses and realize that they are gone forever. We are indebted to those who preserved on film what we were unable to preserve in reality.

Chapter Eighteen

The Hildon Farm

John Arnold McKee was not a farmer. Rather, he was a hard-nosed, successful businessman who used his wealth to fund his passion for yachting, trout fishing, golf, and the dream of owning a stock farm. Born in the village of Rosemont, Ontario in 1859, J.A. McKee had moved rapidly into the world of business and finance. He formed the Dodds Medicine Company in 1899 when he was forty years old, and was also president of Western Steamship Lines. In addition, he sat on the boards of a number of financial institutions. By 1907, the patent medicine company was doing so well, in Europe as well as in North America, that John was able to think about starting his farm. That year he bought 156 acres of farmland on the northwest corner of Bayview and Lawrence Avenues, but seemingly became spooked by the encroaching city and sold his new property just three years after acquiring it. Sir Clifford Sifton would make better use of the place a dozen or so years later when he built three houses for his family that stand there today as part of the Toronto French School. One of these houses was rented by E.P. Taylor and his wife Winifred while they were assembling the land and finances to build their Windfields Farm, a mile or so up Bayview.

In 1910, the same year that John McKee sold his property at Bayview and Lawrence, he bought another farm near the corner of Yonge and Finch. Ironically, this property was even *more* in the path of Toronto's development because of its Yonge Street frontage. Described as the northwest quarter of Lot 18-1E and the southern half of Lot 19-1E, John's new farm reached all the way east to Bayview Avenue. He didn't have much time to enjoy it, since he died two years later at the relatively young age of sixty-two. He left the farm to his son, John William McKee, who had been born on Christmas Day 1897, making him only fifteen at the time.

John William McKee would eventually succeed his father as president of the Dodds Medicine Company and assemble his own impressive array of directorships, both corporate and charitable, but one of the first orders of business for the teenager was the survival of the farm that the family had named "Hildon Farm." Though neither man ever called the farm their primary residence, they did occasionally use it as a summer place, while leaving the day-to-day operations to a farm manager and his staff. While primarily a dairy operation, the farm also produced crops such as hay, oats, and wheat.

Photographer unknown, Toronto Public Library, NY 003.

Hildon Farm on the west side of Bayview Avenue, a little over one-quarter-of-a-mile south of Finch Avenue East, as it appeared in 1916, when many of Willowdale's farmhands were overseas fighting in the First World War.

John William expanded the farm when he bought property on the east side of Bayview Avenue, reaching over to Leslie Street.

John was an avid equestrian and laid out numerous trails on this part of his farm for the Eglinton Hunt Club. By 1923, that encroaching city John Arnold McKee had been worrying about had made farming near Yonge Street an unlikely proposition, and John William McKee sold most of the family's farmland on the west side of Bayview to his brother-in-law, John Norton of the Northbourn Heights Limited Development Company, in order to concentrate his farming efforts on the east side of Bayview.

Northbourn Heights Limited began building houses almost immediately on the western edge of former McKee farmland near Yonge Street, and although they were slowed by the Great Depression and the Second World War, houses were either built or under construction on streets such as McKee Avenue and Norton Avenue, all the way from Yonge Street to Bayview Avenue, by the end of the war.

The Hildon Dairy Farm continued successfully for many years between Bayview and Leslie. The farm was well known in the area, though occasionally for the wrong reasons. Shortly before midnight on October 31, 1937, the main barn on Bayview Avenue caught fire and burned to the ground. Farm manager George Evans, his wife, and two hired hands braved the inferno to save several horses, a bull, and thirty cows. North York firefighters battled through the night to contain the blaze and, while their heroic exertions saved much of the farm's machinery, hundreds of bushels of grain and seventy-five tons of hay were consumed by the flames.

Barn fires were a big deal in those days, before television and the internet, and this one was no exception. At one point over a thousand cars were parked on the narrow roads. Drivers and passengers were arriving, as if from nowhere, to witness the destruction. Many were dressed in Hallowe'en costumes or pajamas. Women in high heels and party dresses stepped gingerly over fire hoses to stand with gentlemen in top hats and tails in the sodden fields — all illuminated by the red-orange glow of the flames, creating a most bizarre scene.

Hildon Farm also attracted national attention, but, ironically, only after it had been abandoned. On September 16, 1952, North York Police, under Chief Roy Risebrough, captured the members of the notorious Boyd Gang in an abandoned McKee barn near Leslie Street, the same barn that had sheltered some of the horses and cows saved from the fire of fifteen years earlier. The Boyd Gang were a little like Toronto's "Bonnie and Clyde," and with their having strayed onto one of the farms of North York, a thumbnail sketch of their exploits seems in order.

Edwin Alonzo Boyd was born in Toronto in 1914, the son of a police officer. After his mother died near the beginning of the Great Depression, he headed west to find work, along with thousands of others. His tale was not unusual and neither was his inability to secure regular employment, so he did what desperate men had done since the beginning of time — he turned to crime. He was caught robbing a service station and spent two and a half years in jail. Upon his release, he returned to Toronto, where he joined a local militia unit. As the situation in Europe worsened, he joined the Royal Regiment of Canada, and was sent overseas where he was involved in several forays into Occupied France. He also served as a motorcycle dispatch rider in England, where he met and married an area woman who worked at the local canteen. The Boyds returned to Toronto several months before the war's end, where Edwin found work as a motorman on the Yonge Street streetcars. On September 9, 1949, he robbed his first bank — the Armour Heights branch of the Bank of Montreal, on the east side of Avenue Road near Haddington Avenue. He robbed six more before being apprehended two years later and sent to the Don Jail.

While in jail, Edwin Boyd became friends with two unrelated criminals named William and Leonard Jackson. The three men escaped on November 4, 1951, and though Willie Jackson was recaptured six weeks later, Edwin and Lennie kept up their crime spree with the addition of new recruit, Steve Suchan. Now known as the Boyd Gang, the three continued to rob banks until Sergeant of Detectives Edmund Tong was shot by the gang on March 6, 1952. He died from his wounds seventeen days later.

The largest manhunt in Canada's history resulted in the capture of all three fugitives, with Steve Suchan and Leonard Jackson caught in a shoot-out in Montreal and Edwin Boyd apprehended at his Toronto residence. The three were returned to the Don Jail, where they were reunited with Willie Jackson. On September 8, 1952, in an almost cinematic turn of events, the entire gang managed to escape *again*. This time would be the last, however, with the redoubled efforts of this latest manhunt involving virtually everyone in town.

The fugitives followed the Canadian National Railway tracks from the jail all the way up the East Don Valley to North York, knowing full well that every step they took could be their last. Splitting up into pairs or working as individuals, they tried to find enough to eat while making their way out of town. George Beauchamp contacted police after a couple of suspicious characters visited his general store in Oriole, at Sheppard and Leslie. Neighbours Owen Cooper and Bob and Howard Trimble also became suspicious as apples disappeared from their orchards, along with vegetables from their gardens. Bob Trimble decided to pay a visit to the old McKee barn, which had been abandoned for some years, although it was still frequented by hobos taking advantage of its proximity to the rail tracks and local teenagers looking for a hangout. He found several straw beds and called the police, who surrounded the barn on September 16 and arrested the fugitives without incident.

This time there would be no escape. Justice was swift and terrible for Steve Suchan, who shot Sergeant Tong, and for Leonard Jackson, who was also at the murder scene. The two men were hanged at the Don Jail on December 16, 1952. Edwin Boyd and Willie Jackson both received "life" sentences. After being granted parole in the mid-1960s, both men moved separately to the west coast, where they lived out the rest of their lives in apparent anonymity. Edwin Alonso Boyd died of pneumonia in British Columbia on May 16, 2002. A feature film documenting his gang's exploits was released ten years later.

Curiosity-seekers swarmed the old McKee barn following the arrests, and before September was over, one of them dropped a lit cigarette that set the straw on fire and burned the barn down to its stone foundation.

Hildon Farm didn't last long, but it sure had some tales to tell the grandkids. The land was sold for the development of Bayview Village in 1954. All that remains today to remind one of the McKees and their farm is McKee Avenue.

Chapter Nineteen

Bud McDougald and Green Meadows

Green Meadows was the last farm in North York. Once covering nearly 300 acres on the eastern halves of Lots 19-3E and 20-3E on the east side of Leslie Street, just south of Finch, the farm had been reduced to less than twenty acres when the accompanying photographs were taken in the spring of 2000. By the end of that summer, nothing remained except the main house. It stands there yet, trapped by seventy-four new "executive" houses that surround the old place like schoolyard bullies.

The land was first granted by the Crown in the early nineteenth century — Lot 20 to Robert Lymburner, and Lot 19 to Francis Brock Jr. on the north half and James Dunton on the south half. These lots ran across the south side of today's Finch Avenue from Leslie Street to the Don Valley Parkway.

Both lots played their part in the early days and both were owned at one time or another by families whose names appear elsewhere in this book. James Johnston hosted the first meetings of the Primitive Methodist Church in his house, on the west half of Lot 20, before Henry Scrace provided land for a permanent church that is still standing on the north side of Finch, just east of Don Mills Road. John Henry, a York councillor in 1856, also farmed the west half of Lot 20, as did Samuel Kennedy, who built a Temperance Hall there in 1878. The Johnston, Scrace, Brock, and Dunton families would continue to own and farm parts of these lots into the 1900s, but the real action didn't start until Bud McDougald bought the property in 1947.

John Angus "Bud" McDougald had been born in Toronto with a silver spoon in his mouth on March 14, 1908, and, though the spoon would be abruptly withdrawn shortly after his twenty-first birthday, he would pay no mind, since by then he was quite capable of buying his own spoons.

Bud's father, Duncan Joseph McDougald (of Scottish ancestry, though the family had been in Canada for several generations by the time Bud was born), was a successful businessman who owned his own investment company known as D.J. McDougald and Company in Toronto. His wealth afforded his son the luxury of an unconventional upbringing. Bud hated school and after being dismissed from Upper Canada College, he was enrolled at St. Andrew's College, where he continued his rebellious ways. Though still a young teenager, he had already founded a small mouthwash company and sold it for a profit.

His next endeavour was even more intriguing. It seems that a Canadian Pacific Railway line connected the northern edge of St. Andrew's Rosedale campus with the western edge of the nearby Thorncliffe racetrack. Bud devised a routine where he would sneak out of school between periods, jump a freight train, and ride it to the racetrack where he would place bets on behalf of his school friends. Since he was still underage, he employed a local riding instructor to actually place the bets. Before long, he made enough money to buy five horses of his own.

Not surprisingly, he didn't have enough time left over to even make a pretense of studying for his exams, and, at the age of fourteen, his formal education came to an end. (In later years he would often joke that he wished he had left school even earlier.) In a bold attempt to salvage something of his son's academic career, Duncan McDougald hired a private tutor to travel with Bud to Europe and wherever else the lad wanted to go. The effort fell short, and when Bud returned to Canada his school days were clearly over. In 1926, at the age of eighteen, Bud went to work, and here his father's connections would prove invaluable.

Bud was hired as an office boy at Dominion Securities, the largest bond dealer in Canada. The company was founded twenty-five years earlier by Edward Rogers Wood, a self-made man from Peterborough who had started out as a telegraph operator at his hometown's Canada Life Assurance office in 1884. He was promoted through the company, moved to Toronto, and struck out on his own when he founded Dominion Securities in 1901. He is also the man who built Glendon Hall in 1925. The 125-acre estate at Bayview and Lawrence would eventually be donated to the University of Toronto by his widow, Euphemia, and, in 1961, it would become the first campus of the brand-new York University.

Moments like this don't come along every day in Canadian financial history — an established titan like E.R. Wood hiring a future titan like Bud McDougald for $30.00 a week to fetch coffee and deliver mail. Although the office position was entry level, young Bud's way of getting to work was anything but. It seems that Duncan McDougald had provided his son with a new Vauxhall automobile and a uniformed chauffeur to drive him to work. After the first few days, young Bud was so embarrassed by all of this that he had the chauffeur drop him off around the corner from the office so he could walk into work like the other office boys. When Duncan got wind of this he offered Bud a choice — either take the car to work and get out at the front door of the office building, or take public transit. Bud hated making a scene at the office, but he hated interacting with the public even more, so from then on the chauffeur dropped him off at the front door.

Once inside, Bud took a real shine to his new job. Finally, here was something he could really sink his teeth into. He took a serious interest in his work, usually staying late to read and learn after everyone else had gone home. He was an apt pupil, often clipping out relevant newspaper articles to leave on his boss's desk and reading all of the company correspondence he could find to educate himself on the inner workings of pending deals. His hard work and intuitive understanding of finance launched him on a rise that can only be described as meteoric. In 1928, he was appointed syndicate manager and put in charge of millions of dollars in investments. The timing couldn't have been better. By the end of next year Duncan McDougald would have lost everything in the October stock-market crash. Bud took a hit like almost everyone else, but kept his position.

In 1934, Bud McDougald married well-known figure skater Maude Eustace Smith, whose skating partner and younger sister Cecil had been the first woman to represent

Canada in an Olympic event when she skated in the 1924 Winter Olympics in France, an Olympics that Maude competed in as well. On his wedding day, Bud was in the middle of a business deal that had fallen through, potentially leaving him $10,000 in debt. He worked the phones throughout his wedding and reception and ended the day in much better financial shape than when he had started. While he was still at Dominion Securities, he was also involved in his own outside interests. By the time 1936 rolled around, Bud McDougald was a wealthy man.

The McDougalds travelled extensively during the 1930s, notably to Britain and Europe, where they bought art and artifacts, as did most of their contemporaries, but Bud's real passion lay in expensive automobiles. He purchased many examples of the finest European marques when they were new or nearly new. The term "classic" had not been applied to automobiles at this point since they were not old enough yet, but Bud's taste was so impeccable that everything he bought would eventually *become* a classic with the passage of time. Lest this be thought of as all too idyllic, it should be mentioned that Bud had his first heart attack in 1938, shortly after his thirtieth birthday. When he recovered he returned to Dominion Securities, where he now controlled all stock trading and where he would remain until the end of the Second World War.

By now Bud McDougald had a reputation as the toughest man in the financial district. Perhaps this was a result of the crash of 1929. Bud had always loved the finer things in life and when the rug was pulled out from under him, he had to search his soul to see if he was willing to do whatever was necessary to get back to the top. Clearly he was.

Bud didn't drink or smoke. He hated being in the public eye and yet his inner circle included some of the most famous people in the world. Kings, Queens, presidents, princes, prin-cesses, and captains of industry all valued his friendship and advice. He was apparently a great storyteller and a loyal and trusted friend. One could assume that he had such a strong inner sense of himself that public recognition was unnecessary. He never spoke on television and only gave a handful of print interviews in his lifetime. The only time he ever spoke on the radio was when he was compelled by the Canadian Radio-television and Telecommunications Commission to publicly state his intentions regarding his involvement in the proposed takeover of an Ottawa communications firm. He spoke for two minutes. In 1945, immediately following the Second World War, Bud would join with Wallace McCutcheon, Eric Phillips, and E.P. Taylor to form a new company that would permanently change the way Canadians do business.

The purpose of the Argus Corporation, as their new company was called, was to gain controlling interest in as many companies as possible, with as little money as possi-ble. This they accomplished by concentrating on key blocks of voting shares, a strategy that worked so well it became a virtual blueprint for Canadian investment firms to this day. By 1964, Argus-controlled companies accounted for 10 percent of all trades on the Toronto Stock Exchange. The companies they controlled included breweries, grocery chains, forestry giants, radio stations, farm equipment man-ufacturers, and even Hollinger Mines, the company that Bud's uncle John McMartin had founded in the early 1900s with his brother and partners, Noah and Henry Timmins and David Dunlap.

By the late 1940s, Bud McDougald had plenty of money to indulge himself in his passions of horse racing and fine automobiles. In 1947, perhaps following the lead of his new partners E.P. Taylor and Eric Phillips, he bought 225 acres on the southeast corner of Leslie and Finch and began construc-tion of his magnificent country estate, Green Meadows.

Photos by Scott Kennedy

The main house and gatehouse at Green Meadows are seen here from Leslie Street on March 31, 2000. The apple trees along the driveway have grown quite wild after going un-pruned for years. The roadways, however, remain unpaved as Bud McDougald intended, although they too are showing the effects of neglect.

The main house stood proudly at the end of a long tree-lined driveway that ran east from Leslie Street. Like Eric Phillips's Wynyates, which stood about a mile south at the corner of Leslie and Sheppard, the main house at Green Meadows was a white-painted brick colonial revival-style mansion. It was far more imposing than its neighbour to the south, for a number of reasons. To begin with, Green Meadows stood boldly at the end of a long drive that was lined with apple trees and white painted fences, while Wynyates was approached from the side and the rear. Secondly, while Wynyates was basically Georgian,

Green Meadows was decidedly colonial revival, adding to the basic Georgian symmetry and simplicity, such details as a tall, porticoed entrance with four columns supporting a triangular pediment. Cut into the pediment was a semi-elliptical fan light decorated with a slender spokes, usually intended to give the impression of a hand fan when opened. At Green Meadows, however, the design is more reminiscent of a delicate spiderweb. This fan-light design, a signature motif for the whole estate, was featured on every building on the property.

The entrance to the main house bears a striking resemblance to Thomas Jefferson's home, Monticello, in Charlottesville, Virginia, which seems ironic, as Bud had little use for politicians in general and even less use for "liberal" politicians like Jefferson.

When the estate was dismantled in 2000, there were still a dozen separate buildings at Green Meadows, with all but the poolhouse, main house, and gatehouse being dedicated to cars or animals. In addition to these three buildings, there was a large indoor arena with stabling in a wing of the building for a dozen Thoroughbreds, garages for approximately thirty cars, a chauffeur's cottage, kennels, greenhouses, and a small multi-purpose building that featured a garage, another stable, and an apartment. When first constructed, the farm would have included a lot more buildings, such as barns to house horses, cattle, farm implements, feed, and other supplies. In addition, more housing would have been required for the hired hands. Typically, the farmhands at these newer estate farms were housed in the original cabins and farmhouses that had been built by previous owners.

Green Meadows included a successful Thoroughbred-breeding operation that produced the first Canadian horses to race in England. The McDougalds' involvement with England didn't end there, however. In 1976, they quietly purchased the historic Kingsclere stables in Hampshire. There, the McDougalds' horses shared stable space with some of the finest Thoroughbreds in the world, including eight derby winners and horses owned by Queen Elizabeth II. Kingsclere's two hundred acres included a magnificent main house, a dozen staff cottages, stabling for eighty-five horses and a long, covered run for stormy days. While in England, the McDougalds enjoyed memberships at Ascot, Epsom, and the Bucks and Turf Club. Members of the Royal family often stayed at Green Meadows when they visited Toronto to attend the Royal Agricultural Winter Fair (where Bud was the president during the 1967 Canadian Confederation centennial year), or the running of the Queen's Plate.

Some might think that this seems like a pretty full life, but the McDougalds would have disagreed. Bud and Maude (or "Jim," as her friends called her), spent most of the winter in Palm Beach in a Mediterranean-style ocean-front mansion. The house, designed by noted Florida architect Addison Mizner, was purchased by the McDougalds from the DuPont family in 1960. Bud maintained that he did just as much business in Florida as he did in Toronto, and had no time to lie in the sun. While in Florida, he was also a governor of the prestigious Everglades Club and oversaw the family's stable of Thoroughbreds, which was moved to Florida every year for the winter racing season.

Back in Canada, Bud was a member of the Mount Royal Club in Montreal, the North York Hunt Club, the Eglinton Hunt Club, the York Club, and the Toronto Club. In the 1940s, he single-handedly rescued the exclusive Toronto Club from bankruptcy and became the club's monitor of properties. One very revealing story from the 1960s took place at the Toronto Club and shows just how wealthy and confident Bud McDougald really was. It seems he was lunching there one day with corporation lawyer and fellow director of Hollinger Incorporated, Percy Finlay, when Percy, exasperated with Bud's endless criticism of the federal government,

Photos by Scott Kennedy

The main house at Green Meadows as it looked on March 31, 2000. The windows in both north and south wings are now hidden behind the unchecked growth of the evergreens.

asked Bud why he thought he had the right to complain so much about his country. Without even glancing around to see who else was in attendance that day, Bud quietly replied, "Because I'm the only man in this room who's paid personal income tax of more than a million dollars every year for the past sixteen years."[1]

In 1966, Bud suffered his second heart attack. This time, he spent the better part of nine weeks, unconscious, in intensive care. It was whispered that he returned to work with a "softened drive," but if this were truly the case, the softening appears to have been minor. In 1969, he took over the directorship of the Argus Corporation from E.P. Taylor, who was now spending much of his time in the Bahamas. It was also in 1969 that Green Meadows was changed forever.

By the late 1960s, North York's rapid growth had surrounded Green Meadows. The borough's politicians were so desperate for new subdivisions and tax revenues that they asked the McDougalds, point blank, if they would sell Green Meadows for housing. The family agreed, on the condition that they were allowed to keep the main house, surrounding outbuildings, and enough land to properly exercise their horses. The politicians agreed, and Green Meadows became one of the last two farms in North York that were allowed to keep livestock. (E.P. Taylor's Windfields Farm on Bayview Avenue was the other.)

Life for the McDougalds appeared to change very little. It must have seemed strange for them to see the lights of other houses through the trees, but they still had their horses, dogs, and cars. They continued to entertain and to travel to England, Palm Beach, and other destinations. Argus continued as a powerful corporate entity and money was never a problem. Although he never confirmed or denied estimates of his personal wealth, Bud was reported to have kept ten-million dollars on hand in cash and gold, out of a total fortune believed to have been in the neighbourhood of a quarter-of-a-billion dollars. He was proud of the fortune that he had built through hard work and personal integrity, and regarded the sons of wealthy men, who became wealthy solely through inheritance, as dilettantes. Still, he dismissed the notion of the self-made man. "All the talk about self-made men is childish, of course. There is always someone else…."[2]

In November 1977, Bud was hospitalized with pneumonia. When he was released from hospital, he and Maude went to Palm Beach to relax and recuperate. He celebrated his seventieth birthday there on March 14, 1978. The next day he was rushed to hospital where he died, following his third heart attack. His body was returned to Toronto where he lay in state at Green Meadows.

His passing was given front page coverage by the *Globe and Mail* on March 16, where he was described as "Canada's most powerful industrialist."[3] The same article quoted author Peter C. Newman, who called Bud McDougald "the central pillar of Canada's business establishment," and General A. Bruce Matthews, a lifelong friend and associate, who described Bud as "very perceptive and unusually skilled." A fellow Toronto Club member recalled "a forceful personality with extreme powers of concentration, an almost feline personality." James Emmerson of the *Toronto Star* agreed, recalling that Bud was "a panther among the potentates of power. While other tycoons roared their way through the financial jungle, McDougald preferred the stealthy, silent approach."[4]

The last word should go to Peter C. Newman, the only journalist Bud seemed to trust, as quoted on page 10 of the *Financial Post* of March 25, 1978: "The dawn of the computer men is with us and even if they manage things slightly more efficiently, they will impart none of the chivalry, daring or Technicolor lifestyle that animated the last chairman of Argus." In fact, things would *not* be managed more efficiently after Bud was gone.

By the end of the year, brothers Conrad and Montegu Black had seized control of Argus, largely by combining the shares their father had left them with the shares they were able to wrest from Maude McDougald and her sister, Eric Phillips's widow Doris. The deal still raises eyebrows today, but, sadly, the brothers' audacity was not to be matched by their acumen. Following Montegu's death, Conrad seemed unable to steer clear of confrontation or controversy, and today the remnants of the once-mighty Argus Corporation lie in long-forgotten shambles.

Photo by Scott Kennedy

The shadow of the main house lurks behind the tree to the right in this March 31, 2000, photo of the chauffeur's cottage and attached garages.

After Bud's death, Maude continued to live at Green Meadows. Her sister, Cecil Hedstrom, came to live with her. The McDougalds didn't have any children so it must have seemed awfully lonely for Maude in the big house with no one but the staff for company before her sister came. For the time being, life would go on much as it had before. The horses remained at Green Meadows, Maude and Cecil still went to Palm Beach in wintertime, and the cars stayed in the garages. By now, virtually all of Bud's cars had become Grand Classics and Maude must have been pestered by offers to purchase any or all of them, but she refused to sell. The cars were a tangible link to her husband, a physical representation of one of his great passions. Who among us wouldn't share her reluctance to sell? One particularly revealing story about Bud's collection was published in the December 2001 edition of the British magazine *Classic and Sports Car*.

In 1991, Mike Fairbairn, a partner in the world-renowned auto auction and restoration company RM Restorations of Chatham, Ontario, was charged with watching over a display of classic cars at the Toronto Auto Show. He tried to strike up a conversation with a young visitor who kept pointing at the cars and saying "we've got one of those."[5] Mike was intrigued, as the lad clearly knew his cars, but every time Mike tried to ask any questions, the boy became quiet and secretive. The next night, the boy returned and explained that it was his job to look after this secret auto collection. Mike continues: "He became worried when I told him that the cars needed more than polish to protect them and finally agreed to let me see them, on the condition that I wouldn't tell anyone."[6]

The boy's directions led Mike to a part of Toronto he knew fairly well. "Among the mid-priced bungalows, I spotted a Tudor (*sic*) gatehouse I'd previously never noticed. Out back was an L-shaped carriage house. When the door opened, the view was stunning — Bugatti Type 35B, Alfa 6C 1750, Isotta Fraschini 8A boat-tail, and this amazing Mercedes."[7] The Isotta Fraschini was a one-of-a-kind speedster with a tulip-wood body, originally built for King Alfonso XIII of Spain. The Mercedes was an Erdmann and Rossi-bodied SSK roadster whose original owner was Rudi Caracciola, Mercedes Benz's top factory racing driver of the late twenties and early thirties. The garage, of course, was at Green Meadows, and the magnificent automobiles were the ones Bud had so lovingly collected and the ones that Maude couldn't bear to sell.

When Maude McDougald died in 1996, the cars were still in their garages. After her death they were donated to the Canadian Automotive Museum in Oshawa, which is affiliated with Sam McLaughlin's estate, Parkwood. Mike Fairbairn had never forgotten what he had seen at Green Meadows that day five years earlier. After visiting the cars at their new home, he was saddened to see that the facility was overcrowded, had a leaky roof, and no budget for restoration or even maintenance of these once-magnificent autos. Mike was eventually able to convince the museum to sell the Mercedes to set up a maintenance fund for the rest of the facility.

The Mercedes was purchased by noted American collector Arturo Keller, and after a meticulous restoration at the RM shops in Chatham, Ontario, the black beauty was awarded "Best of Show" at the Concours d'Elegance in Pebble Beach, California — the most prestigious auto show in the world. Even Bud would have smiled at that.

Green Meadows remained in a state of suspended animation after Maude's death. Finally, in 1999, the remaining thirteen acres were sold to Tiffany Park Homes for a residential development. In the spring of 2000, when the accompanying photos were taken, Green Meadows was abandoned and facing the bulldozers, but it was still quite capable of taking your breath away. The remaining acreage offered plenty of room to ride a Thoroughbred at full gallop. The indoor arena was still the perfect place to exercise the horses in nasty weather, but there were no hoofbeats to punctuate that warm spring day — just the mournful creaking and groaning that can only be experienced in a big, sad, empty old building at the end of its days. Outside, there was no sound, save for the wind through the bare trees. The property was large enough that traffic hustling by on nearby Leslie Street did not break the silence.

There was an overwhelming sadness at Green Meadows during those final days, borne of the realization that soon no one would be able to stand on that grass where horses and cattle once grazed and hear nothing but the wind through the trees, ever again. By summer's end, the trees were gone, bulldozed, cut up, and hauled away, as were the stables, fences, pool house, garages, chauffeur's cottage, arena, and gatehouse.

Photos by Scott Kennedy.

This large building at the very back (east side) of the property, housed the main stables and indoor arena. March 31, 2000.

The main house was spared, but suffered a typical and disrespectful fate when it was forced to serve as the sales office for the subdivision that would replace it. The developer's wife redecorated the main floor to showcase the types of materials the buyers of the new "executive" houses could choose. Unlike many other farmhouses in North York, however, Green Meadows was not demolished after its role as a sales office was fulfilled. In July 2003, the house found sympathetic new owners in Mary Jane Feeley and her husband Brian. The Feeleys set out to give the grand old house the best restoration they possibly could, going so far as to enlist the services of Maude McDougald's former butler, Edward Healey, to ensure the accuracy of the restoration.

Healey was appalled by some of the changes the developer's wife had made and gave the Feeleys the ammunition and inspiration they needed to properly complete the project. When he saw that the entrance hall had been covered in cheap granite, he told Mary Jane that she should get rid of it to reveal the beautiful red-brick floor that was hidden underneath. She took his advice and removed the granite tiles herself. Unlike most people in her position, she did much of the work herself, from simple cleaning and polishing to stripping wallpaper and exterior shutters.

The elegantly curved oak banister in the main hall is worn in a number of spots but as Mary Jane says: "If the Queen Mother touched it, I'm not going to change it."[8] The colours Mary Jane selected for the interior eerily reflected the colours that the McDougalds had used, although she didn't realize this until she had chosen all the colours herself and invited Edward Healey over to see the final result. Thankfully, the Feeleys also chose to retain some of the quirkier, more personal touches that the McDougalds had used to make their house a home, such as the doggie door that allows access to a second-floor porch from the master bedroom and the interior door handles, which stand five feet off the ground in the British style that Bud had insisted on having in his home.

The two Feeley children, a son and a daughter, are the first children to ever live at Green Meadows, a situation that Edward Healey believes would have thrilled Maude McDougald. The daughter's bedroom, where the Queen Mother once stayed, still features the McDougald family crest in the four corners of the ceiling, with its motto, *Vincére vel mort* (victory or death). The Feeleys named their golden retriever "McDougald." Maybe Bud was victorious after all.

CHAPTER TWENTY

The Dunns

SAMUEL DUNN ONCE FARMED 310 ACRES NEAR BAYVIEW AND Finch. His father Jonathan had purchased 110 acres in 1839, fifty acres of Lot 19-1E, and sixty acres of 20-1E, located directly to the north, which he left to Samuel when he died in 1863. By 1892, Samuel had added the western one hundred acres of Lot 19-2E and the northern one hundred acres of Lot 17-2E, that runs east from Bayview Avenue to Leslie Street. When Samuel died, he willed the land to his son, Fred, who farmed until just before the First World War. While it was Jonathan who established the family in North York, it was Samuel who built the beautiful farmhouse and carriage house that stood at 3124 Bayview Avenue until 1995.

The house that Samuel built around 1870 was a standard T-shaped Ontario farmhouse, the plan taken from the popular A.J. Downing book of architectural designs. The attention to detail was anything but standard, however, and elevated the house above many of its contemporaries. Samuel's two-storey house was built of red bricks with yellow brick trim on the corners and over the windows. Contrasting gingerbread trim was installed beneath the eaves. Bay windows were featured on two sides of the house, improving both the exterior appearance

and the interior ventilation. A porch offered shelter from the elements. The house was topped off by a steeply pitched roof and tall, slender chimneys. In its latter years, the house would be painted white with dark shutters. Samuel also built a lovely board-and-batten carriage house at the rear of the farmhouse.

The Dunns farmed this land for over seventy years, from Jonathan's initial land purchases on the west side of Bayview Avenue in 1839 to his son Samuel's purchases on the east side of Bayview in the 1890s, and his grandson Fred's sale of all of their accumulated farmland by the second decade of the twentieth century. The farms on opposite sides of Bayview would face very different fates.

North York didn't actually exist when Fred sold his farmland, but housing developments had already begun to force their way onto former farmland on both sides of Yonge Street. Improved roads and public transportation attracted former city dwellers to the more bucolic environs of the "Toronto Highlands," a name invented by the Model-T-driving real estate agents of the day to describe anything north of Hogg's Hollow. The farms between Yonge Street and Bayview Avenue were quickly gobbled up by developers. Housing developments started spring-

Photo by Patricia Hart, North York Historical Society, NYHS 519.

Shown here in 1964, Samuel Dunn's beautiful farmhouse, which was built in 1870, stood at 3124 Bayview Avenue, until it was demolished in 1995.

ing up on the east side of Yonge Street shortly after the end of the First World War, but their eastward progress was halted by the Great Depression, and again by the Second World War. Following the conclusion of this war, returning servicemen and their new families finally offered up the bonanza of demand the developers had been waiting for, and, by 1947, the post-war housing boom had surrounded Samuel Dunn's farmhouse. To the north, dozens of new houses were under construction on Holmes and Byng Avenues, which now reached all the way to Bayview Avenue. To the west of the house were Dunforest Avenue and Dunview Avenue, while Lawnview Drive now ran north and south across former Dunn pastures behind the house. To the south, McKee Avenue had been cut through to Bayview along the southern border of the Dunns' farmland and the first new houses were under construction. On the east side of Bayview, it was quite a different story.

Concession roads acted a little like windbreaks in those days, as the developers preferred to build out one area at a time so as not to spread themselves too thinly. While the first concession from Yonge Street to Bayview was being inexorably consumed by new houses, the second concession, from Bayview to Leslie Street, remained working farmland. When the Pender family bought Fred Dunn's property on the east side of Bayview, they bought it because they knew it was excellent farmland, not for its development potential. They farmed there until 1918, when they sold the western half of Lot 19-2E to James Fox, who combined the lot with other land he had purchased to build the lovely Kingsdale Jersey Farm, whose story is told in the next chapter. The Foxes farmed here, directly across Bayview Avenue from Samuel Dunn's farmhouse, until 1954, when they sold most of their farm to Farlinger Development Limited. The Bayview Village subdivision currently occupies this former farmland.

The Foxes retained four acres, two houses, and a red barn for their horses. For the next eighteen years, the Foxes gazed across Bayview at Samuel's farmhouse, as the noose of new houses grew ever tighter around both of their necks. By 1972 the Foxes were gone, and in December of that year, their barn and houses were demolished for the construction of the townhouses that currently occupy James Foxway. At least the developer had the decency to acknowledge the past when he named the new roadway. Samuel's farmhouse and carriage house now stood in lonely testament to a vanished way of life. They would stand for a surprisingly long time.

Sympathetic property owners, with enough money to stand their ground, have been the only defence our rural heritage has had against the relentless onslaught of development. Samuel Dunn's farmhouse and carriage house were certainly the beneficiaries of such benevolent ownership. Though they were now situated on the largest piece of private property in the area, their owners were content to pay ever-increasing property taxes and maintenance costs in order to live in a place they loved and felt was worthy of preservation. Still, nothing lasts forever.

Sometime in the mid-1990s, the property fell into the hands of one J.W. Patterson, who decided to cover it in townhouses. Despite the best efforts of many concerned residents, including architectural researcher Julia Gorman, who presented a factual, detailed report that recommended the preservation of the farmhouse and carriage house, the Local Architectural Conservation Advisory Committee decided that townhouses were more important to North York than its rural history. The committee voted in April of 1995 to remove the Dunn property from a proposed inventory of historical properties. Shorn of any protection, the two buildings were torn down and the townhouses went up. The Dunns may not have been one of the more powerful or better-known pioneer families in North York, but their legacy deserved better.

{Chapter Twenty-One}

The Kingsdale Jersey Farm

FOR NORTH YORKERS OF A CERTAIN AGE THIS FARM IS ONE OF the most memorable, for although not a trace remains, the houses, fences, and a beautiful red barn stood right there on Bayview Avenue for all to see until December 1972.

This is one of the farms that many years earlier had surrendered most of its acreage for a portion of Bayview Village, still one of the nicer developments in town, largely because it has somehow avoided being destroyed by monster homes. It's strange to think of a housing development from the 1950s as historic, but the reality is that these houses are now well over fifty years old, as old as the Victorian houses of downtown Toronto were when Bayview Village was constructed. As the city of Toronto ages, it is to the benefit of all to preserve such large, unadulterated neighbourhoods, rather than allowing them to be tossed into the pit of progress.

When the Fox family sold their 297-acre Kingsdale Jersey Farm to Farlinger Development Limited in 1954, they wisely kept four acres, two houses, and a big red barn. This little oasis on the east side of Bayview, just south of Finch, where horses still grazed, was for most people living there at the time, their last glimpse of a way of life that disappeared before they had a

chance to say goodbye. So they said their goodbyes as they passed Kingsdale, pointed it out to their children and new neighbours, took a deep breath, and moved on.

The Foxes weren't the first owners of this land, which includes portions of Lot 18-2E and Lot 19-2E. These lots, like most of the others described in this book were beautiful, rolling pieces of property that included woods, fields, wetlands, and rivers. Originally Crown land grants in the early 1800s, they were full two-hundred-acre farms, bordered by Bayview Avenue in the west and Leslie Street in the east. By the end of the 1800s, however, each had been subdivided along the lines of the river valleys formed by Newtonbrook Creek and the East Don River.

Lot 19-2E was granted by the Crown to John Conn in 1803. Two years later the title would pass to John McLaney and would stay in the McLaney family for a long time, with the entire two hundred acres still owned by the McLaney estate in 1860. The eastern and western halves were leased to two different farmers by the McLaney estate in the 1860s, and the entire lot would come under the ownership of Margaret Sanders, then Henry Sanders, and finally Joseph A. Gould, all in the 1870s. By 1892, John Henry owned the

Photo by Ted Chirnside, Toronto Public Library, TC 126.

Kingsdale Jersey Farm as it appeared in 1955 with a deserted two-lane Bayview Avenue in the foreground. A banquet hall now stands where the barn once stood.

The bungalows of Bayview Village appear to close in on the former Fox family home at 3101 Bayview Avenue in this photo from March 1971.

Photo by Barbara Sabo, North York Historical Society, NYHS 1494.

eastern half of the lot, fronting on Leslie Street, and Samuel Dunn owned the western half, fronting on Bayview Avenue. By 1910, Peter Silas Gibson, son of David Gibson, whose home, as noted earlier, is now the Gibson House Museum, was listed as owner of the eastern half on Leslie Street, with Samuel Dunn's son Fred still owning the west half on Bayview. Later, the Dunn property was sold to the Pender family (also spelled Pinder on some documents).

Lot 18-2E seems to have led a much more exciting life, beginning right off the top with a Crown grant to David William Smith in 1802. David was the surveyor general for York in 1801, and later a member of the Legislative Assembly. Many other well-known local residents would own a piece of the lot at one time or another, including John Finch, who would later run a popular inn at the corner of Yonge and Finch. He owned the west half of Lot 18-2E from 1817 to

Photo by Barbara Sabo, North York Historical Society, NYHS 1508.

This house once stood at 3103 Bayview Avenue, between the barn and the other family house at 3101 Bayview. It is shown here in March 1971, two years before the elegant townhomes of James Foxway would rise on the site of the two farmhouses.

1820. For many years, James Dunton would own the east half of the farm, while Almira Phillips owned the west half. The two men were partners in a sawmill on the East Don River that produced 50,000 board feet of lumber per year.

Martin Flynn, a shoemaker, bought a one-acre portion of the lot on Leslie Street where, along with William Carrick, Jane Roberts, and others who bought small parcels, he started the little hamlet of Flynntown. Flynn's house would stand on the lot from 1858 to 1970 before being relocated by its owners of the time to avoid demolition.

Silas Hill, born in Devonshire, England, was another well-known resident of the lot, acquiring smaller chunks of Lot 18-2E until he owned the reassembled entire western half by 1884, which he left to his son Robert when he passed away in 1896. Robert would farm the property until well into the twentieth century. Even Thomas Clark of Barberry Place got into the act, owning the northwest fifty acres of Lot 18-2E from 1875 until 1884, when he sold it to Silas Hill.

In 1918, James Fox Sr. bought the west half of Lot 19-2E from the Pender family. This was the first piece of the Kingsdale Jersey Farm, which would eventually include parts of Lots 18 and 19, cover nearly three hundred acres of pasture and mixed farming, and include its own dairy. Though James enjoyed horseback riding, he was not a farmer. In fact, he was the general superintendent of O'Keefe Breweries, which would later be owned by E.P. Taylor. James's son John ran the farm, building it into a prize-winning operation, well-known for its beautiful herd of Jersey cows and its immaculate red barns. The herd of sixty-five purebred Jerseys, rare in North York at the time, produced grand champions in Ontario agricultural competitions.

After John died, his brother Jim, who had been working in the United States in the hotel business for ten years, took over the running of the farm and its dairy. Jim and his wife were involved in the community in many other ways as well. The family owned the Filtro Electric Company, Canada's largest manufacturer of coffee percolators and other kitchen appliances. They sponsored the Filtro Electric Perks, a team in the East Toronto Ladies Softball League that won the league championship and were taken by the Foxes to the World Championships in Portland, Oregon, where they finished third. Mrs. Fox also canvassed for the United Way along a route that travelled north to Finch Avenue, east to Leslie Street, and south to Sheppard Avenue, at a time when there were only twelve houses on this entire route. The land in this area was so well-cleared and the countryside so sparsely inhabited that Mrs. Fox was able to watch the traffic lights change at Victoria Park and Sheppard Avenues from her bedroom window, over four miles away. Sadly, the growth of the city was about to become unstoppable.

In 1936, the family closed their dairy, and, in 1954, with the view out of their front windows now filled with houses all the way from Bayview to Yonge Street, Jim and his wife surrendered to the inevitable and closed their farm. Thankfully, they decided to keep four acres right on Bayview, along with one of the barns and two houses. The Foxes would remain there until the end of the 1960s, riding their horses, and running the Filtro Electric Company. After the Foxes were gone, the buildings stood their ground until the end of 1972 when they were reunited with the rest of the farm in a place we can only visit in our memories or imaginations. Today, the townhouses on James Foxway mark the place where two houses and a big red barn stood long enough to offer one last glimpse of a now-vanquished way of life.

Chapter Twenty-Two

From John McKenzie Farm to John McKenzie House

The McKenzie family didn't start farming in Willowdale until relatively late in the nineteenth century, but the home they left behind has become one of the most treasured and well-known in the entire area. Currently the headquarters of the Ontario Historical Society (OHS), this beautifully restored gem combines elements of several styles: notably Queen Anne Revival, Edwardian, and Arts and Crafts. Built in 1913 on Jacob Cummer's original land grant, the house stands as a glowing testament to just how functional and beautiful a heritage building can be in a modern setting. But attaining this status wasn't easy.

English immigrant Philip McKenzie, born in 1824, began farming near Oak Ridges shortly after arriving in Upper Canada sometime in the mid-1800s. In 1865, he married Sarah Thompson of Whitchurch Township in Upper Canada. In addition to being a farmer, Philip was a carpenter, cabinet-maker, and casketmaker by trade. The family farmed in King Township near Oak Ridges until 1884, when they moved south to Willowdale, buying the southern 144 acres of Jacob Cummer's first farm on Lot 18-1E. They moved into a house that Jacob Cummer's son Samuel had built facing Yonge

Street, between today's Parkview and Norton Avenues, in the 1840s. The family got right down to business and soon had a much-admired herd of Holstein cows, as well as pigs and poultry. The farm was successful, neat, and organized.

Philip McKenzie died in 1901 at the age of seventy-seven and left the farm to his third son, John, who married Allie Carson in 1902. Their brief union ended sadly when Allie died the following year. John re-married, this time to Eva Hill, who would eventually outlive him. Together they would raise one son, Phillip, and four daughters, Florence, Ethel, Gretchen, and Jean. As the first decade of the twentieth century drew to a close, however, John began to sense that all was not well with the farm.

By 1910, the face of Willowdale was changing, as more and more homes and businesses were being built on and around Yonge Street. Property taxes were rising, making it harder to operate a profitable farm. The bucolic agricultural lifestyle that the McKenzies had grown up with began to slowly disappear. John decided to be pro-active, and, in 1912, he registered plans for the Empress Subdivision to be built on the family farm — an ambitious project that allowed for 623 houses on new streets stretching all the way over to Bayview Avenue on the farm's eastern border. Other subdivisions were being developed at the same time, and, although it would be years before houses were built as far east as Bayview, early sales near Yonge Street made John McKenzie a relatively wealthy man.

In 1913, John built the current house that stands at 34 Parkview Avenue, then part of his farmland. Two years later, he built a stable to complement a milk house that had been built on the property in 1907. An attached garage was added in 1918. John kept enough of the original farmland to allow his two remaining cows to graze in peace. The Cummer farmhouse, which had stood where the McKenzie House now stands, but facing Yonge Street, was moved several doors east on the newly created Parkview Avenue, and divided vertically to create a semi-detached house.

The house that John built is a strong, expansive structure that draws on a number of different styles to make its own unique statement. The home projects a solid, anchored appearance that betrays its Edwardian roots, with a deep columned verandah, bay windows, and exuberant gables to bring the other two, more decorative styles, into play. The interior of the house has also been restored to its original splendour, and it *is* splendid. White, quarter-sawn oak is used throughout, from chest-high wainscoting to pocket doors, mantelpieces, and beamed ceilings.

Decorative iron radiators still supply even heat, while leaded and stained glass windows add a final touch of elegance. A spacious centre hall greets visitors who pass through the front door and leads to a wide stairway to the second and third floors. The large red-brick house contains twelve rooms, three bathrooms, and several fireplaces. In an extremely prescient move, John also had the house wired for electricity, even though the electrical grid had yet to extend to Willowdale.

Prior to the creation of North York in 1922, the area received its electricity from the Metropolitan Street Railway Company that had been running its radial cars through Willowdale along rails on the east side of Yonge Street since around 1895. The company had built power-generating stations up and down the Yonge Street line to power its cars, and made extra money selling excess electricity to private users. The line was taken over by the Toronto and York Railway Company in 1904, who continued the practice. A proper electrical grid that extended north from Toronto was approaching Willowdale by the time North York was created in 1922. John McKenzie made sure that his home would have power in any event by also installing a gas-powered generator on the west side of the house. Some of the original two-button light switches remain operable throughout the house.

In 1920, John McKenzie retired from farming, keeping only the two cows, and started a building supply business with his older brother George. (Interestingly, William McKenzie, the oldest brother in Philip's family was also involved in the building trade in Willowdale.) The Kingsdale Builders' Supply Company was located on the north side of Kingsdale Avenue in Willowdale, close to Yonge Street. Now John had it all — selling building lots as well as building materials to build the houses on those lots. The company's tiny, one-storey brick office is still in use as an office on the north side of Kingsdale Avenue, though the red bricks are now painted beige and building supplies are no longer part of the equation. After John had a stroke in 1936, the decision was made to close the business.

John McKenzie died in 1941, and was buried in the cemetery of St. John's Anglican Church in York Mills, where both John and his father had served as church wardens. After John's death, Eva continued to live in the house until she died on June 11, 1956. The house was then taken over by John and Eva's eldest daughter, Florence, and her husband, Frank

Photo by Scott Kennedy.

Historic John McKenzie House, located at 34 Parkview Avenue in Willowdale, has served as the Ontario Historic Society's headquarters since 1993. Built in 1913, the large stately structure fittingly turns one hundred as the OHS proudly celebrates its 125th year of service to Ontario. Photo dated 2013.

Brown, who served as the treasurer of the Township of North York from 1931 to 1967. The family sold the house in 1975, and four years later, Florence died.

The house remained a private residence until 1988, when, in anticipation of the massive redevelopment planned for this part of Willowdale, it was sold to developers. The house was abandoned, some of it boarded up, the heat turned off, and the city issued a demolition permit. But nothing happened for almost five years. Some of the pipes burst and local wildlife took up residence in the attic. Plans were unveiled for a ring road that would pass right through the property. Things couldn't have looked much bleaker. Then, the story took a surprising turn.

The Ontario Historical Society, which had been looking for new office space, approached North York City Council to see if there was any chance the McKenzie house could be spared to serve as the society's new headquarters. Development had slowed in Willowdale by this point owing to a "correction" in the local housing market, and, when the historical society caught the sympathetic ear of City Councillor John Filion, good things began to happen. The route of the proposed ring road was moved slightly to the west to avoid the McKenzie property. On August 16, 1993, the Ontario Historical Society signed a twenty-five-year lease with the City of North York and agreed to undertake the restoration and subsequent maintenance of the house, the milk house, the stable, the coach house, and the gardens.

The restoration began under the direction of Dorothy Duncan, the society's executive director, and Rob Leverty, the restoration manager. It was a massive undertaking, costing over $600,000, and involving untold hours spent researching the house and property to make sure that the restoration was as faithful as possible. The project was completed under the most stressful of circumstances, since the area surrounding the house was being prepared for the massive high-rise develop-

ment to follow. All remaining detached houses between the MacKenzie house and Yonge Street were demolished. Every tree between Yonge Street and the house was cut down and the new ring road was bulldozed out of what remained, mere feet from the house itself. Then the pounding began as the footings for the new high-rises were rammed deep into the ground.

The restoration was completed by the spring of 1994, and today it is a spectacular testament to both the original craftsmen who built the house and the dedicated team that brought the magnificence back to life for a new generation. Rob Leverty must have been particularly proud of the accomplishment since he grew up on a farm less than four miles away, near the corner of Leslie and Sheppard. The Leverty farm was located on the west side of Leslie Street, just on top of the hill, north of Sheppard Avenue East on what had originally been McBride family farmland. The Levertys farmed there from the 1930s until 1967, when they surrendered to the encroaching city and moved on.

Today, Rob Leverty is the executive director of the OHS, Dorothy Duncan remains a committed and involved member, and the John McKenzie House continues to charm all those who take the time to visit and participate in the variety of historical activities that take place there. The house is always open during the annual springtime historic tour, *Doors Open Toronto*, and is well worth a visit.[1]

Acknowledgements

Looking back, I can't imagine that I had any realistic expectations of seeing this book in any form other than a one-off volume to satisfy my own curiosity. Still, I plodded along and with the help of the following people, have been granted the privilege of having my name on the book that you now hold in your hands.

My acknowledgements must surely begin where my quest began — in the Canadiana Department of the North York Central Library. Here, on the sixth floor, under the watchful gaze of the life-size golden lion statue that was carved by Paul Sheppard over 170 years ago, I have spent countless hours and photocopy dollars as images of things I saw as a young boy were once again brought to life.

John Jakobson has always been there to offer advice, encouragement, and enthusiasm. He put me in touch with Andrew Lofft and Irena Lewycka, who took the time to help compile the list of the amazing photos that grace these pages. Andrew Lowe and Katherine Pepper provided important genealogical information. Heartfelt thanks are also due to staff and volunteers I have not yet had the pleasure of meeting for the intoxicating array of scrapbooks, photocopies, and indices that were born of many hours of dedicated perseverance.

Thanks must also be given here to members of the North York Historical Society for similar efforts in gathering, compiling, and arranging complex lists of land transactions and other technical assists that I would have been unable to unravel on my own. Donna McLeod and Chris Coutlée of the Toronto Reference Library guided me through the intricate process of preparing all of these images for publication. I will leave the library with special thanks to Ted Chirnside, Lorna Gardner, J.V. Salmon, and the other photographers who captured the disappearance of the farms of North York in their remarkable photographs. Without their passion it would not have been possible to convey these stories to generations who never saw these sights with their own eyes.

Authors, both encouraging and dismissive, have had a profound effect on me. Liz Lundell, whom I actually called on the telephone to seek advice when I first started this project over ten years ago, was most gracious and encouraging, as was publisher John Denison when Liz referred me to him. I have long admired the work of Bill Sherk, Jeanne Hopkins, Harold Hilliard, Ron Brown, and of course, Patricia Hart, whose *Pioneering in North York* must certainly be regarded as the "bible" for all who study the history of North York. Other books, such as Harry Van Oudenaren's absolutely charming, *Bobcaygeon: A Picture Book of Memories*, taught me that you don't have to be a university graduate to convey a sense of place and time. (Harry was a mechanic who came to Canada from his native Holland following the Second World War, and offered a personal history of his adopted hometown as a way of saying "thanks" in 1992.) As for the "dismissive" Toronto history writers — thanks to you too. Your refusal to respond to my earnest enquiries was often all the inspiration I needed.

I must also offer my thanks to Wayne "Hollywood" Joice, who sold me all the pens I needed to complete my long-hand drafts from his corner stall at Queen and Lee.

My family deserves a big thank you, especially my mom who instilled a love of reading in me at an early age, and my better half, Anne Livingston, whose love of history, the natural world, and the written word are a constant inspiration. Anne has also earned my eternal gratitude for handling proofreading and social media duties that are beyond me.

A special thank you also goes to Barry Penhale, publisher emeritus, and Jane Gibson, my editor, who recognized the merit in my work and has gone the distance with me. And special thanks to Britanie Wilson, my copyeditor, and Laura Harris, project editor, at Dundurn Press, who has ensured that all my efforts are all that they should be. And to my fellow North Yorkers and friends, may you enjoy this recreation of the past with an appreciation for all that has gone before.

Notes

BACKGROUND

1. Patricia Hart, *Pioneering in North York* (Toronto: General Publishing Company, 1968) 139.

CHAPTER 1

1. Anne M. de Fort-Menares, "Rendezvous for Radicals," *The Canadian Collector*, Vol. 20, No.1 (January/February 1985): 12.
2. Loyalist flourishes include such architectural details as sidelights and fluted pilasters around the front door, or the wide fascia boards adorned with lengths of parallel mouldings beneath the eaves.
3. Patricia Hart, *Pioneering in North York*, 86.

CHAPTER 2

1. Patricia Hart, *Pioneering In North York*, 169. Hart cites the account as coming from a story by F.A. Mulholland, *The Mulholland Family Tree* (Toronto: Ontario Publishing Company, 1937), 70. The Mulhollands were related to the McBrides by marriage.

CHAPTER 3

1. Jesse Ketchum was born in New York State in 1782, trained as a tanner, but came to Upper Canada at the age of seventeen in 1799. He became involved in real estate, was a politician, and ultimately became a very wealthy man, also known for his generosity. Providing financial support for the building of the first common, school in York, completed in 1818, is but one of his many philanthropic acts. Jesse Ketchum School at 61 Davenport Road is named for him. He died in Buffalo, New York, in 1867. For more information, see the Dictionary of Canadian Biography online: *http://www. biographi.ca/en/bio/ketchum_jesse_9E.html.*

2. Incentive density refers to an arrangement whereby the developer is allowed to build more units on the lot in exchange for something else. In this case, the something else would be the relocation and restoration of the Pease house.

CHAPTER 4

1. Author's Note: As kids we used to play near where the abandoned gypsy wagon once stood just up from a lovely little wetland that we called *Polliwogs' Paradise*, all of which is buried now — so sad.

CHAPTER 5

1. The identity and exploits of the Boyd Gang are detailed more completely in Chapter 17 on the Hildon Farm.
2. The *Willowdale Enterprise*, October 29, 1949, 8.
3. *Ibid*.

CHAPTER 6

1. Information regarding the early ownership of Lot 15-2E comes from a three-ring binder of lot-by-lot land transactions. The original documents were copied to microfilm many years ago. This binder was created as a hard-copy version of the transactions in 1977 by the staff of the North York Public Library, Reference and Research Division of the Canadiana Department.

CHAPTER 7

1. Information involving a Crown land grant to Mary Garner comes from typewritten books of land transaction records, created by the North York Historical Society from original land transaction records, and kept on file in the 6th floor Canadiana section of the North York Central Library. It was not possible to find any additional information on this Mary Garner, or any mention of a husband. Usually it was women married to influential men who received such grants at this time.
2. Len Cullen was also the man who helped Rupert Edwards create the landscaping at Rupert's farm, which would later become Edwards Gardens. This work was undertaken around the same time that Len was trying to establish himself on Sheppard Avenue.

CHAPTER 9

1. The house currently known as the Heinztman House was originally a log cabin built by Crown grantée, Anthony Hollingshead, around 1800. It was enlarged considerably by a subsequent owner in 1817, and again by Charles Heintzman of the Heintzman Piano Company in 1929. Saved from demolition by Markham Township Council and restored as a centennial-year project in 1967, the house is a popular venue for weddings, craft sales, and other events at 135 Bay Thorn Drive in Thornhill. Its story is told more completely in Chapter 11.

CHAPTER 10

1. Dundurn Press of Toronto, Ontario, is keeping Mazo de la Roche's Jalna series in print. For more information, see *www. dundurn.com*.
2. Ronald Hambleton, *Mazo da la Roche of Jalna* (Toronto: General Publishing Co. Ltd., 1966), 217.

CHAPTER 11

1. Doris Fitzgerald, *Old Time Thornhill* (Thornhill, ON: self-published, 1970), 9.

CHAPTER 12

1. Peter Jones, *The Life and Journals of Kah-ke-wa-quo-na-by*, (Toronto: Anson Green, 1860) 70.
2. Background information on Jacob comes from an article by Gladys Allison on page 11 of the *Enterprise* newspaper from June 18, 1953.

CHAPTER 13

1. David Gibson, "Conditions in York County a Century Ago," *Ontario Historical Society Papers and Records*, Vol. XXIV (1927): 256–365.
2. *Toronto Star*, September 10, 1985, N13.

CHAPTER 14

1. Timothy Eaton, born in Ireland in 1834, came to Canada with his brothers in 1854. His first store opened in Kirkton (in the Huron Tract) in 1856. After a brief stint in St. Mary's, Ontario, he opened the store on Yonge Street that provided the foundation of his T. Eaton Co. empire in 1856.

CHAPTER 17

1. *Globe and Mail*, May 15, 1969, 5.
2. *Ibid.*
3. *Toronto Daily Star*, July 8, 1969, 8.
4. *Mirror/Enterprise*, February 2, 1972, 20.

CHAPTER 19

1. Peter C. Newman, *The Canadian Establishment*, Vol. 1 (Toronto: McClelland & Stewart Ltd., 1975), 8.
2. "Who's Who in Business: Canadian Success Story," *Saturday Night Magazine*, Vol. 60, No. 30 (1955): 18.
3. *Globe and Mail*, March 16, 1971, 1.
4. *Toronto Star*, March 16, 1978, A7.
5. Mick Walsh, "From the Cockpit," Classic and Sports Cars, Vol. 20, No. 9 (December 2001): 53.
6. *Ibid.*
7. *Ibid.*
8. *Toronto Star*, December 27, 2003, page L4.

CHAPTER 22

1. Conversations with Rob Leverty, ED, Ontario History Society, and input from Dorothy Duncan contributed to the writing of this chapter.

Bibliography

ARTICLES, BOOKLETS, HANDOUTS, NEWSLETTERS

Begant, Toinette. "A Brief History of the Heintzman House," Thornhill ON: Heintzman House Auxiliary, 2005.

"Blazing a Road to Grandeur," booklet published by the Culture Branch, Department of Parks and Recreation, City of Toronto, 1996.

Boler, Eric. "Foods of Upper Canada." Unpublished essay. Toronto 2011. Scott Kennedy Collection.

de-Fort-Menares, Anne. "Rendezvous for Radicals," *The Canadian Collector*, Vol. 20, No. 1 (January/February 1985): 12.

Duncan, Dorothy. "Gibson House." *The Canadian Antique Collector*, Vol. 8, No. 5 (September/October 1973): 35–37.

Historic Sites in the Borough of North York, Toronto: North York Historical Society, 1971.

"Mr. McDougald's Business." *The Last Post*, Vol. 4, No.4 (January 1975): 27–31.

"Mr. McDougald's House." *The Last Post*, Vol. 4, No. 4 (January 1975): 27–31.

Theimer, Brian, and the North York Historical Board. *Retracing Our Steps: A Tour of a 19th Century Farming Community in the Heart of North York*. Toronto: 1984; revised by the Heritage Section of the Parks and Recreation, Department of the City of North York, 1995.

Walsh, Mick. "From the Cockpit," *Classic and Sports Car*, Vol. 20, No. 9 (December, 2001): 53.

The North York Historical Society Newsletter, September 1992.

The North York Historical Society Newsletter, January–March, 2002.

Wilson, Thomas B. "Some Immigrants in Central Ontario." *The Ontario Register*. Vol. 3, No. 4 (1970): 250.

BOOKS

Austin, D. Rodwell and Ted Barris. *Carved In Granite: 125 Years of Granite Club History.* Toronto: Macmillan Canada, 1999.

Browne, David J., ed. *The Ontario Genealogical Society Directory of Surnames*. Toronto: Ontario Genealogical Society, 1995, 256.

Craig, Gerald M. *Upper Canada: The Formative Years 1784–1841.* Toronto: McClelland & Stewart Ltd., 1966.

Cruikshank, Tom and John de Visser. *Old Ontario Houses: Traditions in Local Architecture*. Richmond Hill, ON: Firefly Books Ltd., 2009.

Delius, Peter, ed. *The Story of Architecture*, Cambridge, UK: Goodfellow and Egan, 1996.

Filey, Mike. *The T.T.C. Story: The First 75 Years*. Toronto: Dundurn Press, 1996.

Fitzgerald, Doris. *Thornhill 1793–1963: The History of an Ontario Village*, Thornhill, ON: self-published, 1964.

_____. *Old Time Thornhill*, Thornhill, ON: self-published, 1970.

Graham, M. Audrey. *150 Years at St. John's, York Mills*, Toronto: General Publishing Co. Ltd. 1966.

Green, Patricia and Maurice, and Sylvia and Robert Wray. *… and they came East to Flamborough*. Waterloo, ON: The Waterdown and East Flamborough Heritage Society, 1997.

Guillet, Edwin C. *Early Life in Upper Canada*. Toronto: University of Toronto Press, 1933.

Legrand, Jacques. Jerome Burne, ed. *Chronicle of the World*. Paris, France: S.A. International, 1989.

Mika, Nick, Helma Mika, and Garry Thompson. *Black Creek Pioneer Village*. Toronto: Natural Heritage Books, 2000.

Hambleton, Donald. *The Secret of Jalna*. Toronto: PaperJacks, a division of General Publishing Co. Ltd., 1972.

Hart, Patricia. *Pioneering in North York*. Toronto: General Publishing Co. Ltd., 1968.

Hopkins, Jeanne. *Bayview Village*. Toronto: Bayview Village Association, 2006.

_____. *The Henry Farm*, Toronto: Henry Farm Community Interest Association, 1987.

Loyal She Remains, Toronto: United Empire Loyalists' Association of Canada, 1984.

Lundell, Liz. *The Estates of Old Toronto*, Erin, ON: Boston Mills Press, 1997.

McCormick, Edwin. *Leading Financial Men of Toronto*. Toronto: self-published, 1912.

McQueen, Rod. *The Eatons: The Rise and Fall of Canada's Royal Family*. Toronto: Stoddart Publishing Co. Ltd., 1998.

Mikel, Robert. *Ontario House Styles*. Toronto: James Lorimer and Co. Ltd., 2004.

Minhinnick, Jeanne. *At Home in Upper Canada*. Toronto: Clarke Irwin and Co. Ltd., 1970.

National Reference Book on Canadian Personalities, 8th edition, 1947–48. Toronto: compiled and published by the Canadian Newspaper Service, Registered 1947.

Newman, Peter C. *The Canadian Establishment*, Vol. 1. Toronto: Seal Book edition by arrangement with McClelland & Stewart Ltd., 1997.

Ondaatje, Kim and Lois Mackenzie. *Old Ontario Houses*. Toronto: Gage Publishing Co. 1977.

Peterman, Michael. *Sisters in Two Worlds:* A Visual Biography of Susanna Moodie and Catherine Parr Traill. Toronto: Doubleday Canada, 2007.

Reaman, G. Elmore. *A History of Vaughan Township*. Toronto: George C.H. Snider, 1971.

Scadding, Henry. Frederick H. Armstrong, ed. *Toronto of Old*. Toronto: Dundurn Press, 1987.

Thompson, Gary. *Village Life in Upper Canada*, Belleville, ON: Mika Publishing Co., 1988.

Tunnell, A.J., ed. *Who's Who in Canada*. Vol. 5, 1949–1951. Toronto: Trans Canada Press, 1951, 691, 945.

Vallee, Brian. *Edwin Alonso Boyd: The Story of the Notorious Boyd Gang*. Toronto: Doubleday Canada Ltd., 1997.

NEWSPAPERS

The Bayview Post:

Editorial, "In Memory of Earl Bales." September 1992.

Hopkins, Jeanne. "In 1968 the cornerstone of Oriole Public School was transferred to Dunlace Public School." July 1995.

Hopkins, Jeanne. "Financier's Estate has played host to Royalty" September 1999.

Hopkins, Jeanne. "Historic family home now slated for demolition." May 2000.

Greco, Julie. "Oldest house in North York to be razed for condos." May 2002.

Hopkins, Jeanne. "Hunt club was forced to move with the times." April 2003.

_____. "Gibson founder celebrated." August 2004.

_____. "Springer house demolished." January 2005.

_____. "Boyd Gang hid in barn." July 2005.

The Don Mills News:

"Bayview Village Biographies." August 6, 1954.

The Enterprise:

"Barn and Silo Destroyed By Fire." November 4, 1937.

"People We Should Know; Roy Risebrough." March 16, 1944.

"People We Should Know; Earl Bales." August 3, 1944.

"Local Veterans' Subdivision Wins Prize in V.L.A. Competition." October 20, 1949.

Allison, Gladys. "The Cummers of Willowdale." June 18, 1953.

"Historic Ridge To Be $9,000,000 Subdivision." June 3, 1954.

Bray, Grace. "Who Are Our Neighbours?" September 21, 1961.

Fitzgerald, Doris. "Historic Steeles Hotel To Go." July 26, 1962.

Chirnside, Ted. "Ye Not So Old North York." July 31, 1963.

Chinsky, Miriam. "Sites of North York: The Gibson House." September 25, 1968.

Bentzen, Phyllis. "Green Bush Inn." April 9, 1969.

"Council Vetoes Green Bush Bid." July 9, 1969.

The Financial Post:

Newman, Peter C. "McDougald: The mark of the man was his style of power." March 25, 1978.

The Globe:

"Death of Joseph Shepard." April 26, 1899.

The Globe and Mail:

"Harold H. Gibson: Surveyor Firm Dated to 1820." May 2, 1946.

Obituary: Donald M. Springer. February 21, 1952.

"Man with 1962 Job Buys 1802 Farmhouse." August 31, 1962.

MacKenzie, James. "Old pub houses roomers." May 15, 1969.

Classified ad for former Mazo de la Roche house. August 12, 1977.

"Financier McDougald, head of Argus Corp., dies at 70." March 16, 1978.

"Dalton Bales killed by car." October 31, 1979.

The Mirror/Enterprise:

Bentzen, Phyllis. "Victim of the wrecking crew." February 2, 1972.

The North York Mirror:

Myers, Jay. "Families showed spirit." December 29, 1976.

Kohane, Jack. "Great-grandson remembers when Gibson House was a home." April 23, 1997.

"Sisters find site of childhood home hard to revisit." May 24, 1997.

"The Dempsey Archivist," September 13, 1997.

Bell, Steven. "Top Canadian financier owned Green Meadows." June 27, 1999.

Skinner, Justin. "Historic old Pease House set for move." February 10, 2002.

Meditskos, Stavroula. "Century-old farmhouse demolished." May 7, 2003.

The North York Post:

Hopkins, Jeanne. "The Joseph Shepard House, The Oldest Building Still Standing in North York." November 1992.

_____. "Rebel sympathizer once owned farm on Yonge." July 2002.

The Richmond Hill Liberal:
Obituary: Samuel Cummer. June 15, 1883.
"The Late Mr. Robert J. Risebrough." September 20, 1928.
"Historic Yonge Street Property Sold For Country Estate." October 31, 1929.

The Telegram:
"Purchase of Nearly 200 acres in North York by R.Y. Eaton." November 23, 1929.
"Lansing to Rouge Hills Highway opens Tuesday." August 19, 1931.
"Mackenzie Hideout Now Becomes Site For Luxury Homes." May 30, 1954.
Fox, Paul. "Historical Upper Canada Home For Sale." August 13, 1962.

The Thornhill Post:
Hopkins, Jeanne. "In 1820 a Thornhill settler, Benjamin Thorne operated the largest flour mill and tannery in Canada." May 1995.
Hopkins, Jeanne. "Originally built from mud brick by a British Colonel in early 19th century, The Heintzman House was home to many prominent Thornhillers." September 1996.

The Toronto Star:
Teskey, Frank. "Green Bush Inn 'too old to restore' but he lives here." June 13, 1968.
"North York won't let students move old inn." July 8, 1969.
Jones, Donald. "Home of Mazo de la Roche is a threatened landmark." May 2, 1976.
Potter, Warren. "Home to be museum." June 4, 1976.
_____. "Owner can't raze writer's home." October 7, 1977.
Emerson, James. "McDougald, the stealthy tycoon." March 16, 1978.
Jones, Donald. "Historical Toronto." March 19, 1979.
Jones, Donald. "Shepard home evokes the past." June 2, 1979.
Evasuk, Stasia. "Our oldest house is still a home." October 21, 1980.
Hilliard, Harold. "Historic home faces demolition." September 11, 1981.
_____. "Pioneer home in path of North York project." April 6, 1982.
_____. "Plan would have school as site of pioneer house." April 27, 1982
_____. "Students give pioneer house a new life." May 3, 1983.
Milne, Lorus. "Don't move Gibson House" (Letter to the editor.) August 30, 1983.
Hilliard, Harold. "Burnings part of colonial wave of terror." September 18, 1985.
_____. "Finch Ave. was named for 19th century keeper of Bird in the Hand (*sic*) Inn." January 7, 1986. (Note: Name was actually "the Bird in Hand Inn.)
_____. "Policeman recalls effortless capture of the Boyd gang." January 28, 1986.
_____. "Anglican sisterhood established convalescent hospital in 1930s." August 5, 1986.
_____. "Historic house to be saved." February 10, 1987.
_____. "North York children in 1920s watched weekly gypsy ritual." April 7, 1987.
Hopkins, Jeanne. "Where did Sheppard Ave. get its name?" August 29, 1991.
Krivel, Peter. "House designated historic site." June 30, 1994.
Brennan, Pat. "Where the rich and famous lived and played." October 14, 2000.
Barnard, Linda. "Historic Home reborn." December 27, 2003.

The West Willowdale Town Crier:
Chinsky, Miriam. "Finding the past in Joseph Shepard House." July 2001.

The Willowdale Mirror:

"Woman bids to save author's home." May 19, 1976.

"Beauty spot envisaged." June 2, 1976.

"Cut trees were obstacle: Engineer." June 15, 1977.

"Famous mansion selling at $600,000." August 17, 1977.

De Giusti, Cos. "De la Roche home will become temple." March 29, 1978.

White, Sheila. "Earl Bales keeps ticking like clockwork." January 9, 1985.

The Willowdale Post:

Whincup, Doris. "Willowdale home was Mazo de la Roche's." June 7, 1972.

REPORTS

"Annual Report 1916." The Association of Ontario Land Surveyors.

"The Gibson House Annual Report," 1964.

"Heritage Structure Report." #Z-79-20. (File for the Samuel Dunn house. City of North York, April 1995.)

Index

About the Author

Photo by Anne Livingston.

Scott Kennedy's first address was R.R. #2, York Mills. He explored and enjoyed the open land of a still mostly rural North York before turning to music at an early age. In 1969, he joined the Toronto Musicians' Association and remained a member until 1995, playing everywhere in Toronto from the Gerrard Tavern to Massey Hall and Maple Leaf Gardens, as well as touring Canada and the United States. His interest in writing found purpose when he was appointed to the board of Animal Alliance of Canada, where he was charged with writing their legislative newsletter, a quarterly publication that was mailed to all provincial and federal members of parliament.

Scott is an award-winning model car builder and slot-car racer, who sold his last "real" old car in 2011 after twenty-nine years of ownership. His involvement in music continues, most recently as bassist and vocalist in the Toronto group *Kensington Market* that formed in Yorkville in 1967. Several years ago, Scott went to the library to borrow a book on the farms of North York and, finding that no such book existed, decided to write one himself. This is his first book. Scott and his partner Anne live with a rotating cast of small mammals, both wild and domestic, in a Heritage Conservation District that they helped create in Toronto's Beaches neighbourhood.